The Bookmark Book

Cut 'n Clip Series

The Bookmark Book. By Carolyn S. Brodie, Debra Goodrich, and Paula K. Montgomery. 1996.

Handy Dandy Reading Records, K-3. Harriet R. Kinghorn. 1996.

The Bookmark Book

Carolyn S. Brodie
Debra Goodrich
Paula K. Montgomery

1996
LIBRARIES UNLIMITED, INC.
Englewood, Colorado

LIBRARIES UNLIMITED, INC.
P.O. Box 6633
Englewood, CO 80155-6633
1-800-237-6124

Suggested cataloging:

Brodie, Carolyn S., 1958-   .
     The bookmark book / Carolyn S. Brodie, Debra Goodrich, and
Paula K. Montgomery.
        Cut 'n clip series.
        viii, 100 p. 22x28 cm.
        Includes bibliographical references (p. 99-100).
        ISBN 1-56308-300-0
        1. Clip art.   2. Bookmarks.   I. Goodrich, Debra. II. Montgomery,
Paula K.
     745.4 1996

Contents

v

Bookmark Timeline

Sources

Book: A. W. Coysh. *Collecting Bookmarkers*. Devon, England: David and Charles, 1974. (A. W. Coysh. *Collecting Bookmarks*. Drake Publishers, 1971.)

Periodical: *Bookmark Collector*, Quarterly from Joan Huegel; 1002 West 25th Street; Erie, PA 16502 $6.00. 1-814-455-8155.

©Carolyn S. Brodie, Debra Goodrich, Paula K. Montgomery

Introduction and Suggestions for Use

A bookmark is simply a flat or semi-flat object, whether paper, leather, fabric, or other flat substance, that is placed between the pages of a book to hold a reader's place. The ubiquitous form may be found in expensive gift stores or it can be made on the spot from a torn piece of paper. When books were first printed with movable type, markers were made of parchment, cloth, or leather. As time progressed, markers were produced of other materials including cloth, paper of different weights and types, silk, silver, and wood. Markers also became Bible scripture reminders and advertisements.

The universal use of bookmarks prompts the examples in this book, which are meant as learning devices for use by students, teachers, librarians, and parents. The information found on the markers has been collected from a wide variety of general reference sources to represent many subjects. Each marker includes either a question or information about a subject that might motivate more reading or further searches for information. On each marker, a suggestion is given to the user to check a particular type of source or to go to the library.

These bookmarks are meant to be copied for use in the classroom, school library media center, public library, or home. Markers may be modified for use in individual situations. A bookmark may become an instructional handout in the library media center as an integrated curriculum lesson. In fact, only the front of each bookmark has been provided with the assumption that each classroom, school library media center, or public library will include its own message on the back of the bookmark such as short bibliographies that note materials in the collection or items available at that location. Assignments or teacher reading lists may be provided on the back of the bookmark. Individual libraries may copy their name, location, and hours of operation on the back or may use a simple rubber stamp to provide public information. Many other uses may be made of the backs or the do-it-yourself bookmarks. For example: awards for work well done, thank you's, rules, origins, book blurbs, alma maters, parent messages, times or hours for specific events, sports schedules, teacher favorites', town histories, directions, lists, spelling words, ads, calendar events, tickets, recipes, biographies of local people, school information, or student designs.

With the availability of copy machines, this simple format is sure to be a subtle information and teaching device. It can become more than just a book marker. It may also become a clue or suggestion to other materials of related interest. This book contains 280 ready-made bookmarks and blank-formatted pages for creative use by the reader. The bookmarks are laid out so that the user may copy and cut once or twice with a paper cutter or scissors. The expense of producing the bookmarks will depend on the color and type of paper or material used.

Materials for Making Bookmarks

photocopier
paper
fabric (cotton, linen, silk, etc.)
leather
envelope corners
metal (silver, copper, brass, tin, pewter, etc.)
plastic
yarn and macramé
wood
dried leaves and flowers
feathers, ivory, and tortoise shell
Post-it™ notes

Associations and Companies As Sources

American Library Association
Children's Book Council
DEMCO
Highsmith
Upstart

WHAT MAKES A GOOD PHOTOGRAPH?

Composition
(Close-ups and long shots)

Decide what is important for your picture. Stand in a spot to get the best angle for your point of view.

Exposure

Learn to use your camera or light meter so that you get the correct amount of light on your subjects.

What are other elements of a good photograph?

Clue: Look for other magazines and books about photography in the Dewey Decimal Classification System section 771 or 778 in your library.

Finger Puppet Pattern

Use this bookmark as a basic pattern for making your own finger puppets. Cut out the two circles. Slip your first finger into one hole and second finger into the other hole. Make your puppet walk or run by moving your two fingers. You may also turn this over and make another puppet on the other side.

There are many books in the school or public library that would give you ideas about making puppets. Can you find stories that you would like to tell using a puppet?

Making Colors

Can you read the word and color it in correctly?

blue
green
yellow
purple
orange
red

Ask the librarian for books about color.

Creating a Paper Airplane

Where can you find more ways to fold paper to make paper airplanes?

Clue: Look in the automated or card catalog or browse shelves in the Dewey Decimal Classification System section 629.133 or 745.592

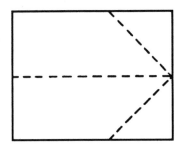

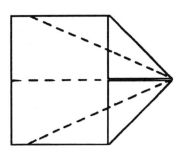

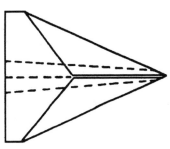

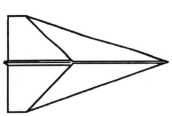

Where can you find information about airplanes?

Clue: Look in the automated or card catalog or browse shelves in the Dewey Decimal Classification System section 629.133

©Carolyn S. Brodie, Debra Goodrich, Paula K. Montgomery

Making an Origami Animal

Can you follow these instructions to make this bird?

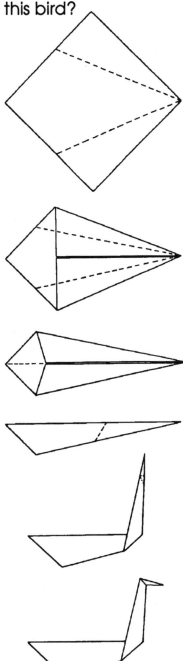

Look for other origami books in the Dewey Decimal Classification System section 736 in your library. You might also look for books about birds.

©Carolyn S. Brodie, Debra Goodrich, Paula K. Montgomery

How to Make Papier-Mâché

Collect these supplies:

Materials for a base such as a balloon, cardboard, cans, styrofoam ball, or wire.
Wheat or wallpaper paste
Newspaper
Water
Buckets or large bowls

Instructions:

Make a mold of the figure that is desired.

Tear four or five large sheets of newspaper into small strips.

Mix paste in a large bowl or bucket according to instructions on the package.

Dip torn strips into the paste. (Don't use too much or the strips will fall apart.)

Mold the strips around the molded figure.

Put on two layers and press to make smooth.

Let the figure dry overnight.

When dry, paint with tempera colors.

Find other art projects by looking in the card or automated catalog in the library.

The Human Skeleton

Are the bones in this skeleton labeled correctly?
Are any names missing?

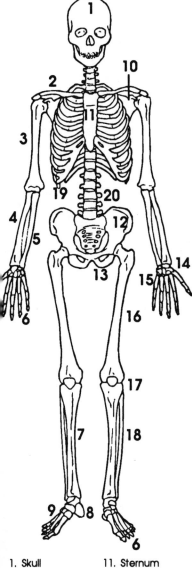

1. Skull	11. Sternum
2. Clavicle	12. Pelvis
3. Humerus	13. Ischium
4. Ulna	14. Carpus
5. Radius	15. Metacarpus
6. Phalanges	16. Femur
7. Tibia	17. Patella
8. Tarsus	18. Fibula
9. Metatarsus	19. Ribs
10. Scapula	20. Vertebra

Clue: Find pictures of human skeletons in books in the Dewey Decimal Classification System section 612.

TEETH

Name these teeth. What is the function of each type of tooth?

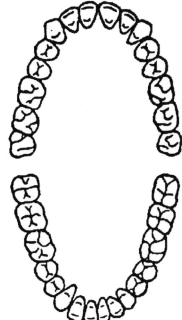

Clue: Look in the vertical file for pamphlets or use encyclopedias for information on types of teeth and their purposes.

THE TOOTH

What does the tooth look like inside?

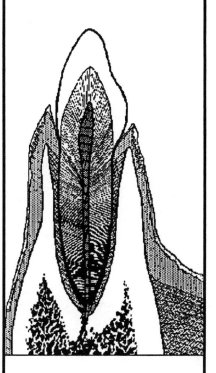

When you have a toothache, what parts of the tooth are affected?

Clue: Use encyclopedias or find a movie about proper dental care.

THE EAR

Trace the path that sound travels in your ear.

Clue: Find other materials in the Dewey Decimal Classification System section 612.

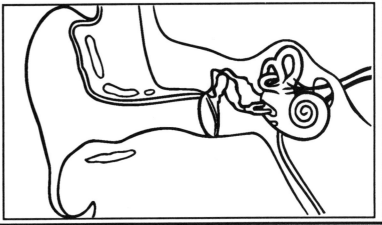

THE EYE

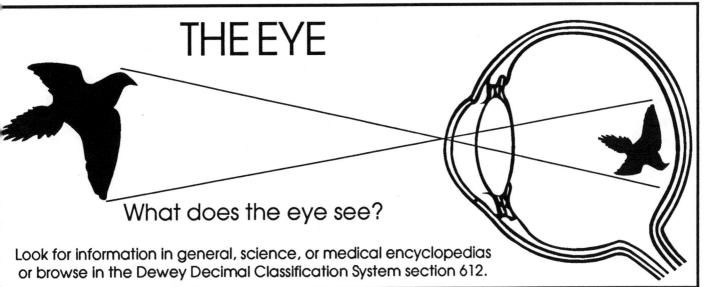

What does the eye see?

Look for information in general, science, or medical encyclopedias or browse in the Dewey Decimal Classification System section 612.

The Nose

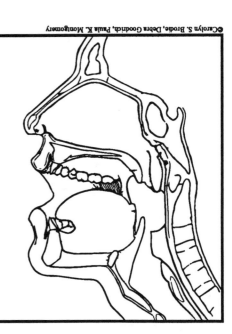

How does the nose work?

Find illustrations of the nose in film or videotapes to find out how your sense of smell works.

The Nervous System

The body has a series of nerves throughout the body. These help the body monitor what is happening in different parts.

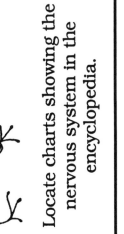

Locate charts showing the nervous system in the encyclopedia.

The Digestive System

Find materials about good health or the human anatomy in the library. Can you find materials that will help you follow the path that food takes through your body?

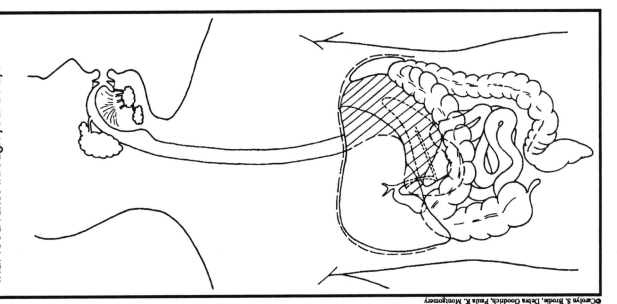

The Circulation System
Trace the blood flow.

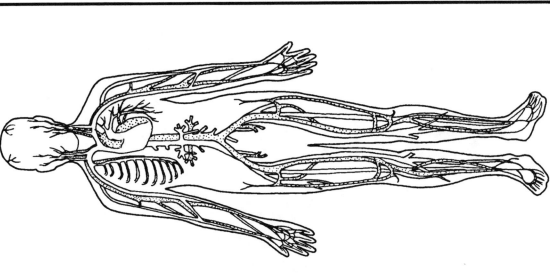

What are veins and arteries?

Clue: Look it up in a dictionary.

Answers: A vein is a vessel through which blood returns to the heart. An artery is a vessel or tube through which blood flows from the heart.

Healthy Snacks

What snacks can you think of that are healthy and nutritious?

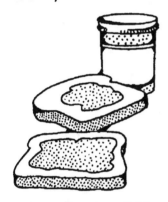

What can you add to a peanut butter sandwich?

Clue: For ideas, browse the Dewey Decimal Classification System sections 641.1 or 641.5. Look in the encyclopedia or in books about nutrition or peanuts. Look at the nutritional information found on a peanut butter jar.

©Carolyn S. Brodie, Debra Goodrich, Paula K. Montgomery

Setting a Table

This is a table setting for an elaborate or special dinner. Which items could be eliminated for a simple lunch?

Use materials about customs to find out more. Use books about decorating for more information about table settings.

©Carolyn S. Brodie, Debra Goodrich, Paula K. Montgomery

Eating with Chopsticks or a Fork

Hold the first chopstick in the hollow of the hand between thumb and first finger. Let the slenderest part of the chopstick rest on the fourth finger. Place the second chopstick against the first and second fingers and hold it with the thumb. Let the ends of the chopsticks meet. Move the two chopsticks together using the first and second fingers to guide them.

Hold the upper back of the fork against the hollow of the hand between the first finger and the thumb. Lay the middle back of the fork against the first and second fingers and hold together with the thumb. The forked portion should be pointed downward.

Where can you find out more about manners?

Clue: Browse the Dewey Decimal Classification System section 395.

©Carolyn S. Brodie, Debra Goodrich, Paula K. Montgomery

IN CASE OF A FIRE

Warn others if necessary.

Feel closed door to see if it is hot before opening it. (If cool, open very carefully; if hot, do not open.)

Kneel or crawl on the ground or floor to breathe as little smoke as possible.

Close doors behind you to slow down the fire.

Move as fast as you can to the nearest safe exit to a place that you have talked about ahead of time.

Stay outside of the burning building until fire officials tell you it is safe.

Call the fire department.

To find out more about fires and fire prevention, use the telephone directory for information about local help. Use the card or automated catalog to find out more about fire prevention.

HOW CAN YOU PREVENT FIRES?

Use a stove only if an adult is present.

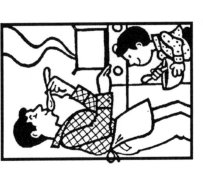

Know where your fire extinguisher is.

✣

Light matches only when an adult is present.

✣

Check to see that the fire detector is working.

✣

Plan a fire exit route in your home with your parents.

✣

Make sure that rags and paper are removed from your house.

✣

Never play with flammable liquids or materials.

Going Out for Trick or Treat?

Go with an adult to well-lit houses or houses of people you know.

Carry a flashlight if it is dark.

Remember traffic rules when crossing the street.

Travel with others, not alone.

Wear flame-retardant costumes in bright colors and use reflector tape on treat bags.

Try to make a costume with make-up rather than a mask so you can see and breathe.

Eat candy and food after it has been inspected by an adult.

How can you find Halloween books in the library media center or library?

Clue: Use the automated or card catalog under HALLOWEEN or HOLIDAYS. You might also look under other subjects such as GHOSTS, WITCHES, COSTUMES, or BATS.

Monday's Child

Monday's child is fair of face,

Tuesday's child is full of ____ ,

Wednesday's child is full of woe,

Thursday's child has far to ____ ,

Friday's child is loving and giving,

Saturday's child has to work for its ____ ,

But a child that's born on the Sabbath day Is fair and wise and good and ____ .

Old Nursery Rhyme

Can you fill in the blanks? Check books of nursery rhymes for the solution.

Phobias

What is the phobia? Can you figure these out?

Phobia	Fear of
Zoophobia	?
?	School
Pyrophobia	?
?	Mice
Dentophobia	?
?	Cats
Acrophobia	?
?	Punishment
Hydrophobia	?
?	Strangers

Use the encyclopedia for answers if you need help.

Superstitions

Superstitions are traditional beliefs about things or events that might tell future events.

Bad luck comes if a black cat walks in front of you.

Bad luck comes from walking under a ladder.

Bad luck comes from breaking a mirror.

Good luck comes from finding a four leaf clover.

Good luck comes if you put a horseshoe over the house door.

Good luck comes from rubbing a rabbit's foot.

Find out more about superstitions in the library.

BIRTHDAY STONES AND MEANINGS

What is your birthstone (ancient or modern) and what does it mean?

JANUARY
Garnet
Constancy

FEBRUARY
Amethyst
Sincerity

MARCH
Aquamarine; Bloodstone
Courage

APRIL
Diamond
Innocence

MAY
Emerald
Love; Success

JUNE
Pearl; Alexandrite; Moonstone
Health

JULY
Ruby
Contentment

AUGUST
Peridot; Sardonyx
Happiness

SEPTEMBER
Sapphire
Clear Thinking

OCTOBER
Opal; Tourmaline
Hope

NOVEMBER
Topaz; Citrine
Fidelity

DECEMBER
Turquoise; Blue Topaz; Zircon
Prosperity

What do the birthstones look like? Check encyclopedias or rock identification books.

©Carolyn S. Brodie, Debra Goodrich, Paula K. Montgomery

Birthday Flowers and Colors

What is your birthday flower and color?

JANUARY
Snowdrop; Carnation
Black; White

FEBRUARY
Primrose
Deep Blue

MARCH
Violet
Silver

APRIL
Sweet Pea; Daisy
Yellow

MAY
Hawthorn; Lily of the Valley
Lavender; Lilac

JUNE
Rose
Pink; Rose

JULY
Water Lily
Sky Blue

AUGUST
Poppy; Gladiolus
Deep Green

SEPTEMBER
Morning Glory
Orange; Gold

OCTOBER
Calendula
Brown

NOVEMBER
Chrysanthemum
Purple

DECEMBER
Holly; Narcissus; Poinsettia
Red

©Carolyn S. Brodie, Debra Goodrich, Paula K. Montgomery

Wedding anniversaries are celebrated traditionally with certain kinds of gifts for the number of years of marriage. Can you fill in the blanks?

First	Paper
Second	_____
Third	Leather
Fourth	Linen, silk, rayon
Fifth	Wood
Sixth	Iron
Seventh	_____
Eighth	Bronze
Ninth	Pottery
Tenth	_____
Eleventh	Steel
Twelveth	Silk
Thirteenth	Lace, textiles
Fourteenth	Ivory
Fifteenth	Crystal
Twentieth	China
Twenty-fifth	_____
Thirtieth	Pearl
Fortieth	_____
Fiftieth	Gold

Can you find the missing answers? Use *The World Almanac and Book of Facts* for answers.

Answers: Cotton; Wood; Tin; Silver; Ruby

Hey diddle, diddle,
The cat and the fiddle,
The cow jumped over
the moon;
The little dog laughed
To see such sport,
And the dish ran away
with the spoon.
Old Nursery Rhyme

Look for other nursery
rhymes in the
Dewey Decimal
Classification
System section
398.

There was an old woman who
lived in a shoe,
She had so many children she
didn't know what to do;
She gave them some broth without any bread;
She whipped them all soundly
and put them to bed.
Old Nursery Rhyme

How many children can you count?

Little Miss Muffet

Little Miss Muffet
Sat on a tuffet,
Eating her curds and
whey;
There came a great
spider,
Who sat down beside
her
And frightened Miss
Muffet away.
Old Nursery Rhyme

What are curds and whey?
Clue: Look for the words
in a dictionary.

12

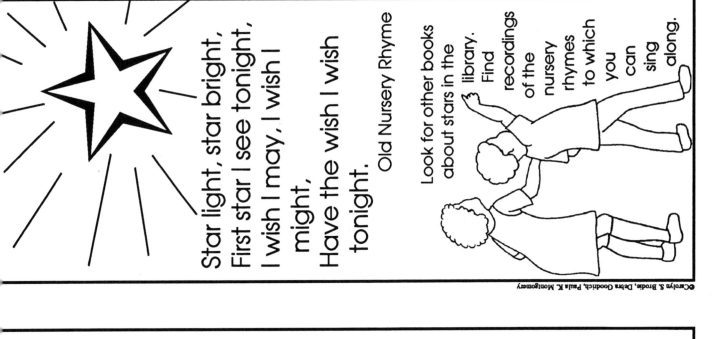

Star light, star bright,
First star I see tonight,
I wish I may, I wish I
might,
Have the wish I wish
tonight.

Old Nursery Rhyme

Look for other books
about stars in the
library.
Find
recordings
of the
nursery
rhymes
to which
you
can
sing
along.

Old Mother Hubbard
Went to the cupboard,
To fetch her poor dog a
    bone;
But when she got there
The cupboard was bare
And so the poor dog had
none.

Old Nursery Rhyme

Who did Mother Hubbard
    visit for her dog?
Look for the nursery
rhyme in Mother Goose
books to find the answer.

Old King Cole
Was a merry old soul,
And a merry old soul was he;
He called for his pipe,
And he called for his bowl,
And he called for his fiddlers three.

Every fiddler he had a fine fiddle,
And a very fine fiddle had he;
Oh, there's none so rare
As can compare
With King Cole and his fiddlers three.
Old Nursery Rhyme.

Look for other Mother Goose rhymes
    in library books.

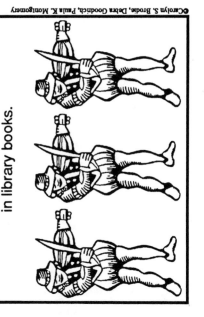

Jack and Jill
Went up the hill,
To fetch a pail of water;
Jack fell down,
And broke his crown,
And Jill came tumbling after.

Old Nursery Rhyme.

There are other verses to this old rhyme. Find the verses in Mother Goose books.

Three blind mice, three blind mice.
See how they run! See how they run!
They all ran after the farmer's wife,
Who cut off their tails with a carving knife,
Did you ever see such a sight in your life,
As three blind mice?

Old Nursery Rhyme.

Can you find books about this rhyme?

Here we go round the mulberry bush,
The mulberry bush, the mulberry bush,
Here we go round the mulberry bush,
So early in the morning.

This is the way we wash our hands,
Wash our hands, wash our hands,
This is the way we wash our hands,
So early in the morning.

This is the way we wash our clothes,
Wash our clothes, wash our clothes,
This is the way we wash our clothes,
So early in the morning.

This is the way we go to school,
Go to school, go to school,
This is the way we go to school,
So early in the morning.

Old Nursery Rhyme.

Sing along to a recording of this and other nursery songs. Listen to the recording in your library.

14

Jump Rope Rhyme

I had a little turtle,
His name was Tiny Tim,
I put him in the bathtub
To see if he could swim.
He drank up all the
   water,
He ate up all the soap;
He died last night
With a bubble in his
   throat.
How many flowers did
   he have?
1, 2, 3, etc.

Practice this rhyme with your jump rope. You may find other rhymes in books in the Dewey Decimal Classification System section 398.8 in the library.

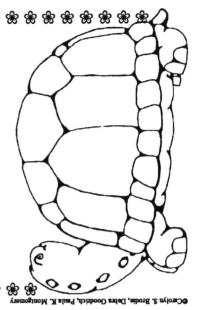

Jumping Rope?
Try this one.

Teddy Bear, Teddy Bear,
turn around
Teddy Bear, Teddy Bear,
touch the ground
Teddy Bear, Teddy Bear,
shine your shoe
Teddy Bear, Teddy Bear,
how old are you?
1, 2, 3, 4, etc.

Can you find other jump rope rhymes in the library? Try making up your own verses.

Pat-a-cake, pat-a-cake,
   baker's man,
Bake me a cake as fast as
   you can;
Pat it and prick it, and
   mark it with a B,
Put it in the oven for Baby
   and me.

Old Nursery Rhyme.

Look for other books of hand rhymes and finger plays in the library.

15

J O K E S

"Jimmy is sick today and he can't come to school."

"Who is calling?"

"This is my father."

"This is the tenth mistake you have made this morning. How can you make so many in one day?"

"I get up early!"

DRIVE OTHERS CRAZY!

Find more joke books in the Dewey Decimal Classification System section 793.7.

Proverbs

A proverb is a well-known saying giving an idea or truth. Here are some sayings to ponder.

Don't cry over spilled milk.

Don't put the cart before the horse.

Don't count your chickens before they're hatched.

A penny saved is a penny earned.

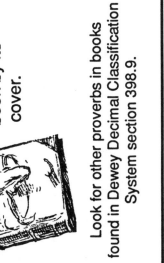

Don't judge a book by its cover.

Look for other proverbs in books found in Dewey Decimal Classification System section 398.9.

Tongue Twisters

Try saying these fast if you dare!

The sixth sick sheik's sixth sheep's sick.
(*Guinness Book of World Records* says this is the most difficult tongue twister in the world.)

She sells seashells by the seashore.

Rubber baby-buggy bumpers.

Tom three Tim three thumbtacks.

Use the card or automated catalog to find books of riddles and tongue twisters.

Riddles

What is orange and falls off walls? *Humpty Pumpkin.*

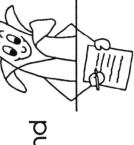

What is yellow and writes? *A yellow banana.*

Which side of a peacock has more feathers? *The outside.*

Think up your own riddles or find riddle books in the library.

Riddles

How do you fit six elephants in a Volkswagon? *Three in the front, three in the back.*

Why do elephants have trunks? *Because they don't have glove compartments.*

What is gray, has four legs and a trunk? *A mouse going on vacation.*

You can find many more riddle books in the library. Use the card or automated catalog to help in your search.

Knock Knock Jokes

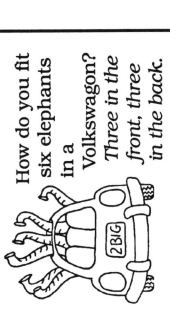

Knock Knock.
Who's there?
Dora Belle.
Dora Belle who?
Dora Belle is broken, so I knocked.

Knock Knock.
Who's there?
Toledo.
Toledo Who?
It's easy Toledo a horse to water, but you can't make it drink.

Knock Knock.
Who's there?
Dexter.
Dexter who?
Dexter halls with boughs of holly.

More knock knock jokes can be found in the Dewey Decimal Classification System section 793.7 or 808.882.

17

What do these instruments have in common? What class of instruments are they?

For clues, use an encyclopedia or a musical reference source.

Answer: Strings

Can you identify these woodwind instruments? If you need help, look in an encyclopedia or musical reference source.

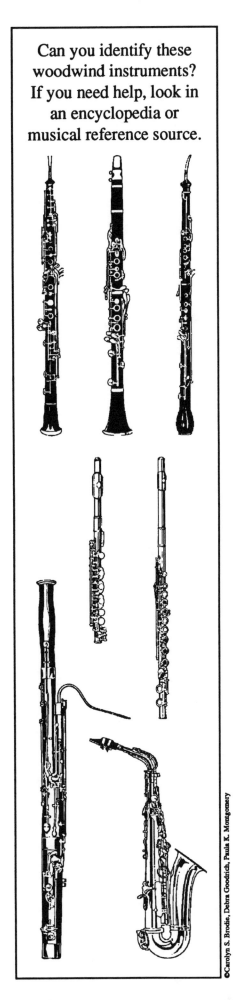

What parts of the body do all of these brass instruments require for playing?

For clues, browse in music books found under the Dewey Decimal Classification number, 781 or 784.1.

Answer: hands (fingers) and mouth

What class of instruments are these and what do they often provide in musical pieces?

Use encyclopedias or musical reference sources for clues.

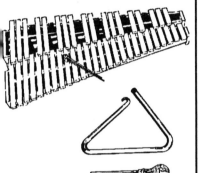

Answer: Percussion; Rhythm

©Carolyn S. Brodie, Debra Goodrich, Paula K. Montgomery

What do these instruments have in common?

Use encyclopedias and musical dictionaries for clues.

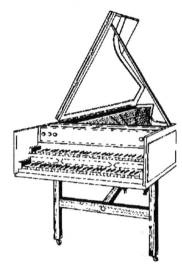

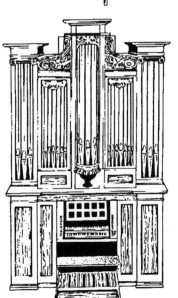

©Carolyn S. Brodie, Debra Goodrich, Paula K. Montgomery

VOICES
Who sings high and who sings low?

soprano
contralto
tenor
alto
bass

What kind of videotapes can you locate that help you understand the difference in the sounds that these voices make?

Use your library.

©Carolyn S. Brodie, Debra Goodrich, Paula K. Montgomery

19

MUSICAL ELEMENTS

Write the correct letter of the meaning of each word on the line beside the word.

_____ 1. Tone

_____ 2. Rhythm

_____ 3. Melody

_____ 4. Harmony

a. A musical arrangement of notes in time.

b. A sequential arrangement of notes to make a phrase.

c. A sounding together of three or more notes.

d. A musical sound of a definite pitch.

Clue: Use an encyclopedia or musical dictionary for help with the answers.

Answer: 1-d; 2-a; 3-b; 4-c

MUSICAL TERMS

Can you speak in musical terms? How would you use these words?

Tempo

Staff

Sharp #

Presto

Octave

Meter

Measure

Legato

Key

Flat ♭

Crescendo

Clef 𝄢

Chord

Andante

Allegro

Clue: Use a musical dictionary to find definitions and examples of use.

WHO ARE THESE COMPOSERS?

Clue: Look for biographical or musical encyclopedias and dictionaries.

Answer: Beethoven, Mozart, Handel, Bach, Haydn

NUMBERING SYSTEMS

ROMAN	ARABIC
I	1
II	2
III	3
IV	4
V	5
VI	6
VII	7
VIII	8
IX	9
X	10
XX	20
XXX	30
XL	40
L	50
LX	60
C	100
D	500
M	1000

What is XCIX?

Can you keep going? Find help in books about numbers or use encyclopedias and almanacs.

Answer: 99

Measurements

If you want to find the number of

?

in

?:

LENGTH
millimeters in inches,
multiply inches by 25

meters in yards,
multiply yards by .9

kilometers in miles,
multiply miles by 1.6

VOLUME
liters in pints,
multiple pints by .47

liters in quarts,
multiply quarts by .95

WEIGHT
grams in ounces,
multiply ounces by 28

ounces in grams,
multiply grams by .035

If you want other conversion rates, check in an almanac or encyclopedia for information.

Geometric Shapes

Match the name with the shape.

square

circle

rhombus

rectangle

triangle

trapezoid

parallelogram

pentagram

hexagram

Use the card or automated catalog to find books and videotapes about geometry.

Fractions

Which fractions are equivalent?
Look at the shaded areas of each pie graph.
Which shaded areas are the same?

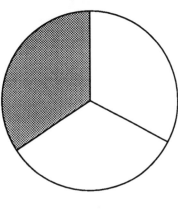

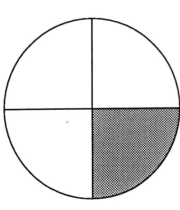

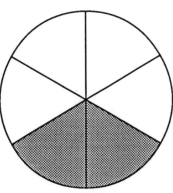

Find other books about fractions in the card or automated catalog.

DECIMALS

Common fractions reduced to decimals and rounded off to the nearest thousandths

1/2	=	.5
1/3	=	.333
1/4	=	.25
1/5	=	.2
1/6	=	.166
1/8	=	.125
1/16	=	?
1/32	=	.031
2/3	=	?
3/4	=	.75

Use the almanac to find more information about decimals.

METRIC CHART

LINEAR MEASURE
10 millimeters (mm) =
   1 centimeter (cm)
10 centimeters =
   1 decimeter (dm) =
   100 millimeters
10 decimeters =
   1 meter (m) =
   1,000 millimeters
10 meters =
   1 dekameter (dam)
10 dekameters =
   1 hectometer (hm) =
   100 meters
10 hectometers =
   1 kilometer (km) =
   1,000 meters

FLUID VOLUME MEASURE
10 milliliters (ml) =
   1 centiliter (cl)
10 centiliters =
   1 deciliter (dl) =
   100 milliliters
10 deciliters =
   1 liter (l) =
   1,000 milliliters
10 liters =
   1 dekaliter (dal)
10 dekaliters =
   1 hectoliter (hl) =
   100 liters
10 hectoliters =
   1 kiloliter (kl) =
   1,000 liters

WEIGHT
10 milligrams (mg) =
   1 centigram (cg)
10 centigrams =
   1 decigram (dg) =
   100 milligrams
10 decigrams =
   1 gram (g) =
   1,000 milligrams
10 grams =
   1 dekagram (dag)
10 dekagrams =
   1 hectogram (hg) =
   100 grams
10 hectograms =
   1 kilogram (kg) =
   1,000 grams
1,000 kilograms =
   1 metric ton

Find other books and materials in the Dewey Decimal Classification System section 510 in the library.

Finding the Area

Circle = Multiply the square of the diameter by .785398.

Rectangle = Multiply the length of the base by the height.

Square = Square the length of one side.

Triangle = Multiply the base by the height and divide by 2.

Trapezoid = Add the lengths of the two parallel sides, multiply by the height, and divide by 2.

Look for more information about geometry in the card or automated catalog.

©Carolyn S. Brodie, Debra Goodrich, Paula K. Montgomery

Finding the Circumference

To find the circumference of a circle, multiply the diameter by 3.14159265 or π.

Can you find the circumference of the earth?

The sun?

The moon?

An official basketball?

An official baseball?

An official golf ball?

Use an encyclopedia to find the diameter of these spherical objects.

©Carolyn S. Brodie, Debra Goodrich, Paula K. Montgomery

Finding the Volume

Cone

Multiply the square of the radius of the base by 3.1416 (π), multiply by the height, and divide by 3.

Cube

Cube the length of one edge.

Cylinder

Multiply the square of the radius of the base by 3.1416 (π) and multiply by the height.

Pyramid

Multiply the area of the base by the height and divide by 3.

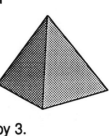

Sphere

Multiply the cube of the radius by 3.1416 (π), multiply by 4, and divide by 3.

Find the formulas for other objects by using mathematical books in the Dewey Decimal Classification System section 516.

©Carolyn S. Brodie, Debra Goodrich, Paula K. Montgomery

U.S. Currency Values

One dollar = four quarters

One dollar = ten dimes

One dollar = twenty nickels

One dollar = one hundred pennies

Find out how your money works. Find books in your library about money or coins.

COOKING MEASUREMENTS

16 tablespoons = 1 cup

12 tablespoons = 3/4 cup

8 tablespoons = 1/2 cup

4 tablespoons = 1/4 cup

2 tablespoons = 1/8 cup

1 tablespoon = 1/16 cup

2 cups = 1 pint

2 pints = 1 quart

4 quarts = 1 gallon

3 teaspoons = 1 tablespoon

48 teaspoons = 1 cup

Practice cooking measurements by using cookery books located in Dewey Decimal Classification System section 641.5 in the library.

Equivalents

Draw a line between those items that are equivalent.

Clue: Use dictionaries, almanacs, or encyclopedias for help in figuring out the answers.

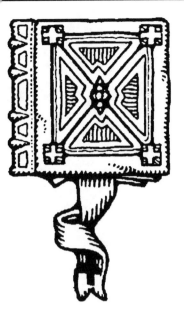

Dewey Decimal Classification System 000-099

Browse here if you are looking for:

General Works	000
Bibliography	010
Library Science	020
Encyclopedias	030
Periodicals	050
Organizations	060
Journalism	070
General Collections	080
Manuscripts & Rare Books	090

Dewey Decimal Classification System 100-199

Browse in this section if you are interested in:

Philosophy & Psychology	100
Ontology & Methodology	110
Knowledge, Cause, Purpose & Man	120
Pseudo- & Parapsychology	130
Specific Philosophic Viewponts	140
General Psychology	150
Logic	160
Ethics	170
Ancient, Medieval, & Oriental Philosophy	180
Modern Western Philosophy	190

Dewey Decimal Classification System 200-299

Browse in this section if you are interested in these topics.

Religion	200
Religion (general)	210
Bible	220
Christian Doctrinal Theology	230
Christian Moral & Devotional Works	240
Theology Christian Pastoral, Parochial, Etc.	250
Christian Church	260
Christian Church History	270
Christian Denominations & Sects	280
Other Religions	290

Dewey Decimal Classification System 300-399

Browse this section if you are interested in these topics.

The Social Sciences	300
Statistics	310
Political Science	320
Economics	330
Law	340
Public Administration	350
Social Welfare	360
Education	370
Public Service	380
Customs & Folklore	390

©Carolyn S. Brodie, Debra Goodrich, Paula K. Montgomery

Dewey Decimal Classification System 400-499

Browse in this section if you are interested in these topics.

Language	400
Linguistics & Nonverbal Language	410
English & Anglo-Saxon	420
Germanic Languages	430
French, Provencal, Catalan	440
Italian, Romanian, Etc.	450
Spanish & Portuguese	460
Latin & Other Italic Languages	470
Classical Greek	480
Other Languages	490

©Carolyn S. Brodie, Debra Goodrich, Paula K. Montgomery

Dewey Decimal Classification System 500-599

Browse in this section if you are interested in these topics.

Sciences	500
Mathematics	510
Astronomy & Allied Sciences	520
Physics	530
Chemistry & Allied Sciences	540
Earth Sciences	550
Paleontology	560
Anthropological & Biological Sciences	570
Botanical Sciences	580
Zoological Sciences	590

©Carolyn S. Brodie, Debra Goodrich, Paula K. Montgomery

Dewey Decimal Classification System 600-699

Browse in this section if you are interested in these topics.

Technology (Applied Sciences)	600
Medical Sciences	610
Engineering	620
Agriculture	630
Home Economics	640
Business & Related Enterprises	650
Chemical Technology	660
Manufacturing	670
Assembled & Final Products	680
Buildings	690

Dewey Decimal Classification System 700-799

Browse in this section if you are interested in these topics.

The Arts	700
Civic & Landscape Art	710
Architecture	720
Sculpture & The Plastic Arts	730
Drawing & Decorative Arts	740
Painting & Paintings	750
Graphic Arts	760
Photography	770
Music	780
Recreation	790

Dewey Decimal Classification System 800-899

Browse in this section if you are interested in these topics.

Literature	800
American Literature in English	810
English & Anglo-Saxon Literature	820
Germanic Languages Literature	830
French, Provencal, Catalan Literature	840
Italian, Romanian, Etc., Literature	850
Spanish & Portuguese Literature	860
Latin & Other Italic Languages Literature	870
Classical & Greek Literature	880
Literature of Other Languages	890

©Carolyn S. Brodie, Debra Goodrich, Paula K. Montgomery

Dewey Decimal Classification System 900-999

Browse in this section if you are interested in these topics.

General Geography & History	900
General Geography, Travels, Description	910
Collective Biography	920
Individual Biography	92 or B
Ancient History	930
History of Europe	940
History of Asia	950
History of Africa	960
History of North America	970
History of South America	980
History of Islands & Polar Regions	990

From the Card or Automated Catalog to the Shelf

First, search your card or automated catalog in a number of ways, depending on what you want to find:

Name of author, illustrator, or person responsible for a work;

Name of a person as a subject;

Subject of interest to you that is a major descriptor of information or a keyword;

Title of a work or series of works; or

Call number (optional in some systems).

Second, search the catalog.

Third, find the description for an item that is of interest to you.

Fourth, print or copy the call number of the item on a piece of paper.

Fifth, go to the general numbered area of shelves.

Sixth, find the item by call number, which should be arranged in numeric order on the shelf.

Finally, use the item in the library or check it out.

Dewey Decimal Classification System

000–099 GENERALITIES
(encyclopedias, bibliographies, periodicals, journalism, computers)

100–199 PHILOSOPHY AND RELATED DISCIPLINES
(philosophy, psychology, logic)

200–299 RELIGION

300–399 SOCIAL SCIENCES
(economics, sociology, government, law, education, careers, customs, folklore)

400–499 LANGUAGE
(language, dictionaries, grammar)

500–599 PURE SCIENCES
(mathematics, astronomy, physics, chemistry, geology, paleontology, biology, zoology, botany)

600–699 TECHNOLOGY AND APPLIED SCIENCES
(medicine, engineering, agriculture, home economics, business, radio, television, aviation)

700–799 THE ARTS
(architecture, sculpture, painting, music, photography, recreation, games, and sports)

800–899 LITERATURE
(novels, poetry, plays, criticism)

900–999 GEOGRAPHY, HISTORY, BIOGRAPHY, AND RELATED DISCIPLINES

Browse with the Dewey Decimal Classification System. Locate subjects of interest to you.

Reasons to Read a Book

❦

Pleasure

❦

Enjoyment

❦

Information

❦

Book Reports

❦

Recipes or
instructions for
doing something

❦

Curiosity

❦

Science fair
projects

❦

*And So Much
More...*

Caring for Books and Materials

To take good care of your books, try these suggestions:

Keep your hands clean when using books.

Keep pages straight (not bent).

Use a bookmark (do not lay the book upside down on a table).

Turn pages from the top, not the bottom.

Keep books out of wet weather.

Keep books away from animals and small childen who don't know what books are.

Can You Find These Parts of a Book?

Which Is Which?

Spine
with Call Number

Book Jacket

Blurb

Title Page

Copyright Page

Preface

Table of Contents

Glossary

Appendix

Index

How does each
book part
help you find
information?

Test-Taking Tips

- ✓ Don't wait until the last minute to study.

- ✓ Use the last night before to review and then get a good night's sleep.

- ✓ Try to practice making up questions that you think might be on the test.

- ✓ Ask a study buddy questions about the material or tell someone about what you have learned.

- ✓ Try to teach the material to someone else.

- ✓ Take all materials that you will need to the test location.

- ✓ Read or listen to the instructions and make sure that you understand them.

- ✓ Read all multiple-choice answers before making a decision.

- ✓ If you don't know an answer, skip to another question. Go back later.

- ✓ Check your answers if there is time.

For more study and test-taking help, find Dewey Decimal Classification System section 371.3.

Kinds of Test Questions

Knowing the kind of questions that may be on a test can help you study.

ESSAY
Example: Write a paragraph about the life cycle of a frog.

MULTIPLE-CHOICE
Example: Circle the most correct answer.
A frog
a. is a cold-blooded reptile.
b. breathes with gills during its entire life cycle.
c. usually begins its life as a fertilized egg in water.
d. none of the above.

FILL-IN-THE-BLANK
Example: Fill in the blank with the best answer.
Most frogs eat _____.

TRUE OR FALSE
Example:
Most frogs are aquatic, but some live on land, in burrows, or in trees.

MATCHING
Example: Draw a line to connect the word with the correct phrase.
1. tadpole   a. organ for breathing
2. insect   b. early stage of life
3. lung   c. frog food

Clue to answer questions: Use an encyclopedia.

Reading and Books

"…The difference that beautiful books can make in a life: a tradition still carried on by many; a tradition which I hope will never cease for the young, whose passion for books may ever spawn new dreams."
Myra Cohn Livingston

"I had just taken to reading. I had just discovered the art of leaving my body to sit impassive in a crumpled up attitude in a chair or sofa, while I wandered over the hills and far away in novel company and new scenes…. My world began to expand very rapidly,… the reading habit had got me securely."
H. G. Wells

"I am sure I read every book of fairy tales in our branch library, with one complaint—all that long golden hair. Never mind—my short brown hair became long and golden as I read and when I grew up I would write a book about a brown-haired girl to even things up."
Beverly Cleary

Use reference books of quotations to find more in your library.

Good Listening Tips

Make yourself comfortable.

Concentrate on what is being said.

Remove other distractions.

Listen for word cues that indicate important ideas.

Clarify points by asking questions.

Take notes if necessary.

Think about what will be heard beforehand.

Find recordings in the library for listening practice.

MINI-BOOK REPORT FOR INFORMATION BOOK

After reading an information book, answer the following:

Author:

Title:

Publisher and Date:

Topic of the Book:

Important Facts:

My Opinion:

Mini-Book Report for Fiction

After reading a book, answer the following:

Author:

Title:

Publisher and Date:

Summary of the Plot:

My Opinion:

Homonym:

a word that sounds the same as another word, but has a different spelling and meaning

see	sea
made	maid
dear	deer
flee	flea
herd	heard
hare	hair
son	sun
scent	cent
flower	flour
peak	peek
pain	pane
rain	rein
bear	bare
rap	wrap
wring	ring

Use a dictionary or thesaurus for other words.

Antonym:

a word that means the opposite of another word

hard	soft
up	down
create	destroy
heavy	light
far	near
full	empty
big	small
hot	cold
push	pull
close	open
front	back
same	different
dry	wet
smooth	rough

Use the dictionary or thesaurus for more words.

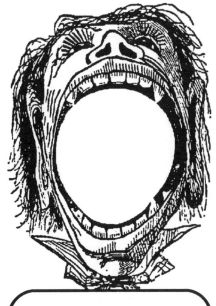

Mispronounced Words

Here are some words that are frequently mispronounced. Correct pronunciations are listed for each word. Can you think of other words that are often mispronounced?

access	AK *sehs*
accurate	AK *yuhr iht*
alias	AY *lee uhs*
chef	*shehf*
column	KAYHL *uhm*
corps	*kawr*
docile	DAHS *uhl*
drowned	*drownd*
figure	FIHG *yuhr*
infamous	IHN *fuh muhs*
maintenance	MAYN *tuh nuhns*
picture	PIHK *chuhr*
salmon	SAM *uhn*
subtle	SUHT *uhl*
suede	SWAYD
vehement	VEE *uh muhnt*

Use a dictionary for correct pronunciations of other words about which you are unsure.

Using a Dictionary

A dictionary is a book or is in electronic format. There are many different kinds of dictionaries. Some contain everyday words and some common technical terms. Specialized dictionaries contain words used in a particular field or subject area.

A dictionary often includes:
- word entries
- pronunciation
- syllabication
- part of speech
- synonyms or antonyms
- definition
- example of word use
- quotations using the word
- other forms of the word
- usage notes
- etymology

Examine the different kinds of dictionaries found in your library.

Using a Thesaurus

A thesaurus is a book or in an electronic format. It lists synonyms and antonyms. It helps you find interesting words when writing.

For example: beautiful
synonyms—fair, lovely, ravishing, gorgeous, pretty
antonyms—ugly, unattractive, repulsive, unsightly

Find a thesaurus in your library and locate these words:
lost
witch
princess
enchant
fantasy
pretend

USING A TABLE OF CONTENTS

A table of contents usually appears in the front of a book. It outlines in consecutive order the sections that can be found within the book.

How can you use a table of contents?

It will help you decide whether or not you are interested in the contents.

It will help you find out whether or not the information you need is in the book.

It will give you an outline of what the author thought was important.

It will give you an idea about the main and subordinate topics in the book.

It will help you find the page numbers for certain topics in the book.

Find several books in the library with a table of contents.

An Index

An index is a list of the topics in a book with the page or location number. It is usually in alphabetical order and found on a page in the back of the book.

Example:

Game	21-29
Computer	23
History	22, 41
Hobby	24

See also Sports;
  Recreation
Game Fishing
  See Fishing

©Carolyn S. Brodie, Debra Goodrich, Paula K. Montgomery

An Atlas

An atlas is a collection of maps. It can be used for locating places, planning trips, and finding out information about places. There are both general atlases and specialized atlases.

To use an atlas you must:
find places on the maps
measure distances
use direction
use map symbols

Locate atlases in the library and practice your skills.

©Carolyn S. Brodie, Debra Goodrich, Paula K. Montgomery

Common Misspellings
These words are often misspelled.
Can you think of other words you often misspell?

achievement
acquaintance
acquire
anxiety
benefit
bureau
cafeteria
challenge
curiosity
discipline
except
fascinating
guarantee
height
icicle
initial
journal
leisure
miniature
ninety
occasional
perceive
receipt
ridiculous
scissors
thoroughly
utilize
vacancy
weird

Find a dictionary or a book on correct usage of words.

©Carolyn S. Brodie, Debra Goodrich, Paula K. Montgomery

Reading a Newspaper Article

Lead

Details

More Details

Most newspaper articles contain a lead that answers who, what, where, when, and why. Following the lead are more details to explain the answers to the questions.

Find the newspapers in your library and locate an article with a good lead.

How to Prepare an Outline

Title
I. First main idea about the subject
  A. First supporting subtopic
    1. First fact supporting subtopic A
      a. First detail supporting fact 1
        (1) First minor detail supporting detail a
        (2) Second minor detail supporting detail a
      b. Second detail supporting fact 1
    2. Second fact supporting subtopic A
  B. Second supporting subtopic
    1. First fact supporting subtopic B
    2. Second fact supporting subtopic B
II. Second main idea about the subject
  A. First supporting subtopic
  B. Second supporting subtopic
  C. Third supporting subtopic

Use this format for organizing information on subjects you find in the library.

Other Ways to Report on a Book

Book Jackets
Bumper Stickers
Cards
Cartoons
Dioramas
Drawings
Finger Puppets
Flannelboard Story
Journals
Letters
Mobiles
Murals
Oral Reports
Poetry
Postcards
Recipes
Skits
Songs
Time Lines
Time Capsules
Videotapes

Look for craft and activity books in the library for other book extension ideas.

35

Parts of Speech

Match the part of speech with the correct or best definition.

Part of Speech

_____ 1. noun
_____ 2. pronoun
_____ 3. verb
_____ 4. adjective
_____ 5. adverb
_____ 6. preposition
_____ 7. conjunction
_____ 8. interjection

Definition

a. describes a noun or pronoun
b. relates to a noun or pronoun and another word in a sentence
c. names a person, place, or thing
d. tells more about a verb, adjective, or adverb
e. takes the place of a noun
f. connects words or groups of words
g. expresses strong feeling
h. expresses action or state of being

Clue: Use a dictionary to help with the definitions

©Carolyn S. Brodie, Debra Goodrich, Paula K. Montgomery

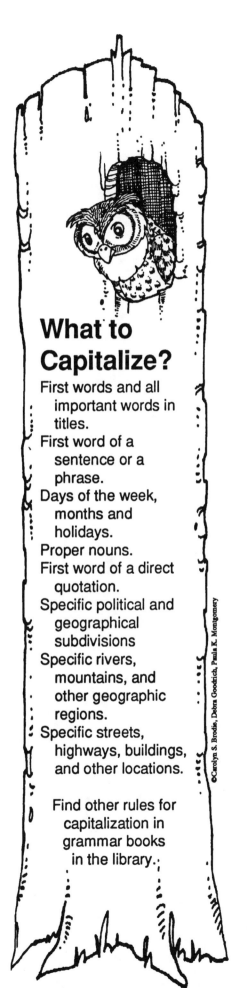

What to Capitalize?

First words and all important words in titles.
First word of a sentence or a phrase.
Days of the week, months and holidays.
Proper nouns.
First word of a direct quotation.
Specific political and geographical subdivisions
Specific rivers, mountains, and other geographic regions.
Specific streets, highways, buildings, and other locations.

Find other rules for capitalization in grammar books in the library.

©Carolyn S. Brodie, Debra Goodrich, Paula K. Montgomery

What to Punctuate?

Use commas:
*for separating the day of the month, or a special day from the year.
*after the greeting in a formal letter.
*after the closing in a formal letter.
*between words or phrases in a series.
*to set off groups of digits in large numbers.
*to separate unrelated numbers in a sentence.
*to set off words or phrases that suggest a break in thought.

How do you use a period, an apostrophe, an ellipse, a semicolon, a colon, a hyphen, a dash, a virgule, quotation marks, question marks, exclamation marks, brackets, and parentheses?

Find answers in grammar books in the library!

©Carolyn S. Brodie, Debra Goodrich, Paula K. Montgomery

Largest, Smallest

What is the largest...

Planet in the Solar System?

State in the United States?

What is the smallest...

Planet in the Solar System?

State in the United States?

Use the almanac or *The Guinness Book of World Records* to find answers to these and other questions.

Highest or Tallest

Who is the tallest man?

What is the highest mountain?

What is the highest temperature?

What is the tallest building in the United States?

Use the almanac or *The Guinness Book of World Records* to find the answers to these or other questions.

Hot or Cold, Wet or Dry?

Hottest temperature?

Coldest temperature?

Wettest place on earth?

Driest place on earth?

Use the almanac or *The Guinness Book of World Records* to find answers to these and other questions.

Common Tools for Working with Wood

Woodworkers use these tools to make things. What can you do with each tool?

Find books about woodworking in your library using Dewey Decimal Classification System section 684.

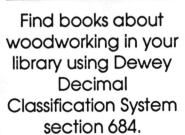

Common Cooking Utensils

Which tools would you use in the kitchen for cooking?

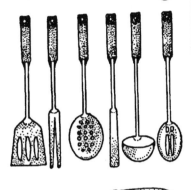

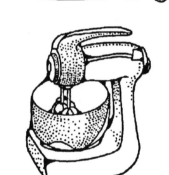

Find books about cooking in the library using Dewey Decimal Classification System section 641.5.

Common Tools for Gardening and Farming

What can you do with each of these tools?

Find materials about gardening in your library using Dewey Decimal Classification System section 635.

Be Jolly in January!
Read about…

NATIONAL HOBBY MONTH

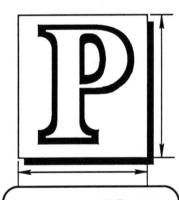

INTERNATIONAL PRINTING WEEK

HAT DAY

…in your library.

Frolic in February!
Read about…

BLACK HISTORY MONTH

AMERICAN HEART MONTH

INTERNATIONAL FRIENDSHIP WEEK

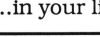…in your library.

Make Merry in March!
Read about…

MUSIC IN OUR SCHOOLS MONTH

THE START OF SPRING

NATIONAL AGRICULTURE WEEK

…in your library.

Acclaim April!
Read about...

INTERNATIONAL GUITAR MONTH

JEWISH HERITAGE WEEK

ARBOR DAY

...in your library.

Hurray for May!
Read about...

BIKE SAFETY MONTH

NATIONAL PET WEEK

LAW DAY

...in your library.

Jump for June!
Read about...

THE SUMMER SEASON

NATIONAL ROSE MONTH

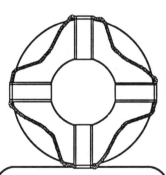

NATIONAL SAFE BOATING WEEK

...in your library.

Enjoy July!
Read about…

NATIONAL PARK & RECREATION MONTH

SPACE WEEK

NATIONAL ICE CREAM DAY

…in your library.

Applaud August!
Read about…

AMERICAN ARTISTS APPRECIATION MONTH

BALD EAGLE WEEK

NATIONAL RELAXATION DAY

…in your library.

Celebrate September!
Read about…

AUTUMN'S ARRIVAL

HISPANIC HERITAGE MONTH

FARM ANIMALS AWARENESS WEEK

…in your library.

Observe October!
Read about…

COMPUTER LEARNING MONTH

THE WORLD SERIES

NATIONAL MAGIC WEEK

…in your library.

News in November!
Read about…

INTERNATIONAL DRUM MONTH

NATIONAL CHEMISTRY WEEK

GENERAL ELECTION DAY

…in your library.

Delight in December!
Read about…

UNIVERSAL HUMAN RIGHTS MONTH

NATIONAL ROOF OVER YOUR HEAD DAY

WINTERY WEATHER

…in your library.

Famous African Americans

Each of these African Americans was involved in a special endeavor. What did they do?

Dred Scott
Estevanico
James Forten
Ralph Bunche
Crispus Attucks
Harriet Tubman
Sojourner Truth
Phillis Wheatley
Denmark Vesey
Jackie Robinson
James Beckworth
P. B. S. Pinchback
Benjamin Banneker
Frederick Douglass
Jean Baptiste DuSable
Booker T. Washington
Guion Stewart Bluford Jr.
George Washington Carver
Martin Luther King, Jr.
Madame C. J. Walker
Marian W. Edelman
Thurgood Marshall
Marian Anderson
Matthew Henson
W. E. B. Du Bois
Louis Armstrong
Langston Hughes
Duke Ellington
Paul Robeson
Charles Drew
Rosa Parks
Jesse Owens
Scott Joplin
Ida B. Wells
Malcolm X

Use biographical reference materials to find out more in your library.

Famous Hispanic Americans

Each of these Hispanic Americans was involved in a special endeavor. What did they do?

Isabel Estrada
Efren Herrera
Johnny Rodriguez
Luis Tiant
Orlando Cepeda
Roberto Clemente
Jose de Diego
Jose Feliciano
Rita Moreno
Luis Munoz Rivera
"Chi-Chi" Rodriguez
Jose Ferrer
George Santayana
Cesar Chavez
Eugenia Maria de Hostos
Herman Badillo
Luis Munoz Marin
Henry Cisneros

Use biographical reference materials to find out more in your library.

Famous Asian Americans

Each of these Asian Americans was involved in a special endeavor. What did they do?

Chen Ning Yang
Laurence Yep
Ed Young
Yoshiko Uchida
Taro Yashima
Hideyo Noguchi
Isamu Noguchi
D. S. Saund
Nancy Kwan
Peter Quay Yang
I. M. Pei
Tsung Dao Lee
Kristi Yamaguchi
Minoru Yamasaki
Maya Ying Lin

Use biographical reference materials to find out more in your library.

Famous Native Americans

Each of these Native Americans was involved in a special endeavor. What did they do?

Massasoit
Sacagawea
Tecumseh
Pocahontas
Pontiac
Hendricks
(a Mohawk chief)
Sequoyah
John Ross
Crazy Horse
Sitting Bull
Stand Watie
General Ely S. Parker
Sarah Winnemucca
Chief Joseph
Susan LaFlesche Picotte
Geronimo
Quanah Parker
Jim Thorpe
Ella Deloria
Maria Tallchief
Buffy Sainte-Marie
Wilma Mankiller
Vine Deloria

Use biographical reference materials to find out more in your library.

©Carolyn S. Brodie, Debra Goodrich, Paula K. Montgomery

Famous Women

Each of these women have made important contributions. What did they do?

Eleanor Roosevelt
Rosa Parks
Elizabeth Cady Stanton
Margaret Wise Brown
Margaret Sanger
Louisa May Alcott
Harriet Beecher Stowe
Dolley Madison
Elizabeth Blackwell
Florence Nightingale
Harriet Tubman
Laura Ingalls Wilder
Marian Anderson
Susan B. Anthony
Ida Wells Barnett
Rachel Carson
Babe Didrickson
Amelia Earhart
Mary Harris Jones
Wilma Rudolph
Elizabeth Seton
Sojourner Truth
Phillis Wheatley
Mary Cassatt
Clara Barton
Mary Pickford
Jane Addams

Use biographical reference materials to find out more in your library.

©Carolyn S. Brodie, Debra Goodrich, Paula K. Montgomery

NEWBERY AND CALDECOTT MEDALS

The Newbery Medal is awarded annually to the author of the most distinguished contribution to American literature for children published in the United States during the preceding year. There are no limitations as to the character of the book considered except that it be original work. Honor Books may be named. These shall be books that are also truly distinguished.

The Caldecott Medal is awarded annually to the artist of the most distinguished American picture book for children published in the United States during the preceding year. There are no limitations as to the character of the picture book except that the illustrations be original work.

The awards are restricted to writers who are citizens or residents of the United States.

The committee in its deliberations is to consider only the books eligible for the Awards, as specified by the above terms.

The Newbery and Caldecott Medals are awarded by the Association for Library Service to Children of the American Library Association.

©Carolyn S. Brodie, Debra Goodrich, Paula K. Montgomery

Famous Discoveries

What year were these discoveries made?

Adrenaline	John Jacob Abel
Bacteria	Anton van Leeuwenhoek
Blood Circulation	William Harvey
Cells	Robert Hooke
Cholera Bacteria	Robert Koch
Evolution by Natural Causes	Charles Darwin
Fermentation Causes	Louis Pasteur
Halley's Comet	Edmund Halley
Laws of Motion	Isaac Newton
Neutron	James Chadwick
Oxygen Isolated	Joseph Priestley
Pluto	Clyde W. Tombaugh
Planetary Motion	Johannes Kepler
Radioactivity	Wilhelm Roentgen
Relativity	Albert Einstein
Symbolic Logic	George Boole
Uranus	William Herschel

For the answers to the question look in the almanac or the encyclopedia.

Famous Inventors

What are these people famous for inventing?

Thomas Edison
Alexander Graham Bell
Eli Whitney
Robert Fulton
George Washington Carver
John Deere
Marie Curie
Rudolph Diesel
George Eastman
Bill Gates
Enrico Fermi
Henry Ford
Garrett Morgan
Wilbur and Orville Wright
Robert Goddard
Louis Pasteur

Look for answers in the almanac or in the encyclopedia or in a biography in your library.

INVENTIONS That Influenced History

When were these invented and who was the inventor?

Airplane
Aspirin
Coca-Cola
Computer(s)
Cotton Gin
Dynamite
Frozen Food
Holograph
Laser
Lawnmower
Microwave Oven
Motorcycle
Phonograph
Polio Vaccine
Rifle
Tape Recorder
Telescope
Toilet (flush)
Typewriter
Zipper

Look for answers in the almanac or in the encyclopedia in your library.

Playing Marbles

How to Play Pots

Make a circle on the ground.

Put the marbles that you will risk inside the circle.

Each player shoots in turn from outside the circle.

The player keeps all the marbles that are knocked outside the circle.

The player gets another turn if the marble stays inside the circle.

There are many other ways of playing marbles. Find out about these from books in the library.

Playing Hopscotch

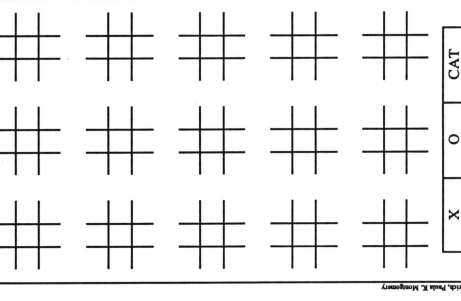

Draw a chalk figure on the pavement with nine numbered compartments. Each compartment should be bigger than your feet. (A stick may be used to draw the figure in the dirt.)

Stand in front of the first step, toss a pebble or marker into the compartment.

Hop on one foot over space one to space two.

Hop on one foot to space three.

Hop on both feet to space four and five at the same time. (One foot should be in four and one foot in five.)

Hop on one foot to space six.

Hop on both feet to space seven and eight at the same time. (One foot should be in seven and eight at the same time.)

Hop on one foot to space nine.

Hop on both feet out of nine.

Return counting backwards.

While standing on one foot in space two, pick up the pebble and hop onto one and out.

Stand in front of space one and throw the pebble or marker into space two.

Begin the hop again.

If you miss the square with the pebble, you lose your turn. If you put both feet down or your feet are on a line, you lose your turn. The first person to finish a round trip, wins.

Find other ways to play this game in the library.

Playing Tic-Tac-Toe

Two players play this game. One chooses an "X" and the other "0." Players take turns making their mark on the board. To win the player must have three marks in a row (horizontally, vertically, or diagonally). If neither player wins, the cat wins.

X		
O		
CAT		

Use the card or automated catalog to find other pencil and paper games.

Halls of Fame

Write for information on these sports.

National Baseball Hall of Fame and Museum, Inc.
P.O. Box 590
Cooperstown, NY 13326

Naismith Memorial Basketball Hall of Fame
P.O. Box 179
1150 West Columbus Avenue
Springfield, MA 01101-0179

National Bowling Hall of Fame and Museum
111 Stadium Plaza
St. Louis, MO 63102

College Football Hall of Fame
5440 Kings Island Drive
Kings Island, OH 45032

Pro Football Hall of Fame
2121 George Halas Drive, N.W.
Canton, OH 44708

National Soccer Hall of Fame
11 Ford Avenue
Oneonta, NY 13820

Use the almanac to find out star sports players inducted into halls of fame.

©Carolyn S. Brodie, Debra Goodrich, Paula K. Montgomery

What Was the Olympic Sport of These Americans?

Bruce Jenner

Dorothy Hamill

Mark Spitz

Bonnie Blair

Jesse Owens

Carl Lewis

Greg Louganis

Janet Evans

Eric Heiden

Dan Jansen

Florence Griffith-Joyner

Kristi Yamaguchi

Jackie Joyner-Kersee

Peggy Fleming

Dick Button

Use an almanac to collect the facts that will help you answer this question.

©Carolyn S. Brodie, Debra Goodrich, Paula K. Montgomery

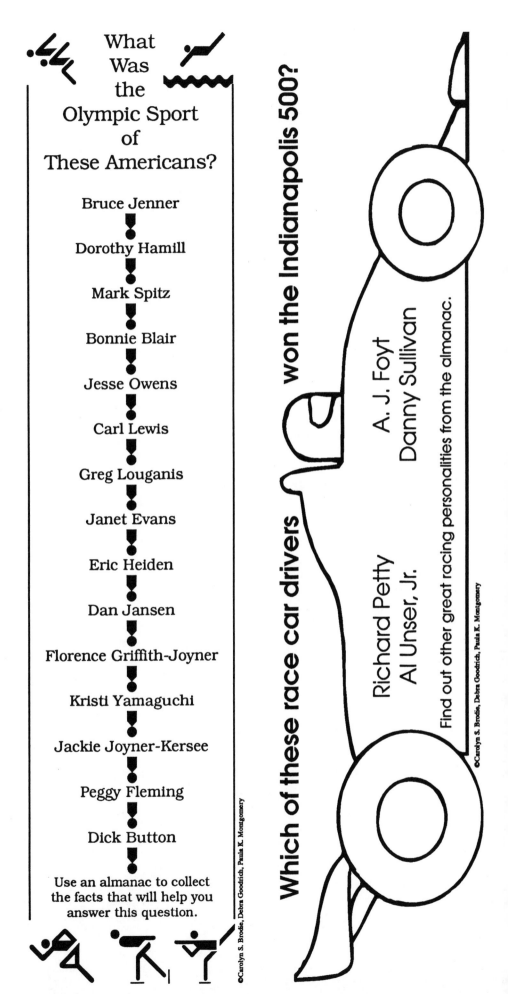

Which of these race car drivers won the Indianapolis 500?

A. J. Foyt
Danny Sullivan

Richard Petty
Al Unser, Jr.

Find out other great racing personalities from the almanac.

©Carolyn S. Brodie, Debra Goodrich, Paula K. Montgomery

The Basketball Court

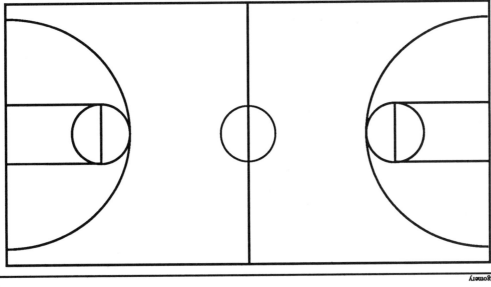

What are the dimensions of the court?

Where are the baskets?

Find the answers in the encyclopedia.

National Basketball Association Teams

Atlanta Hawks
Charlotte Hornets
Cleveland Cavaliers
Denver Nuggets
Golden State Warriors
Indiana Pacers
Los Angeles Lakers
Milwaukee Bucks
New Jersey Nets
Orlando Magic
Phoenix Suns
Sacramento Kings
Seattle SuperSonics

Boston Celtics
Chicago Bulls
Dallas Mavericks
Detroit Pistons
Houston Rockets
Los Angeles Clippers
Miami Heat
Minnesota Timberwolves
New York Knickerbockers
Philadelphia 76ers
Portland Trail Blazers
San Antonio Spurs
Utah Jazz

Washington Bullets

• • •

Find the address of your favorite team in the almanac. You can read more about basketball in books found in Dewey Decimal Classification System section 796.323.

SOCCER

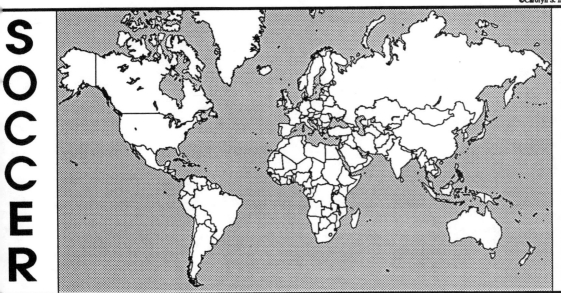

Which countries in the world have teams that played in the most recent World Cup? Which country won?

Find out more about this sport by finding books in your library.

National Hockey League

MIGHTY DUCKS OF ANAHEIM
BOSTON BRUINS
BUFFALO SABRES
CALGARY FLAMES
CHICAGO BLACKHAWKS
DENVER AVALANCHE
DETROIT REDWINGS
EDMONTON OILERS
FLORIDA PANTHERS
HARTFORD WHALERS
LOS ANGELES KINGS
MINNESOTA NORTH STARS
MONTREAL CANADIENS
NEW JERSEY DEVILS
NEW YORK ISLANDERS
NEW YORK RANGERS
OTTAWA SENATORS
PHILADELPHIA FLYERS
PITTSBURGH PENGUINS
ST. LOUIS BLUES
SAN JOSE SHARKS
TAMPA BAY LIGHTNING
TORONTO MAPLE LEAFS
VANCOUVER CANUCKS
WASHINGTON CAPITALS
WINNIPEG JETS

How do you play this game?

Find out more about this sport from books in the library. Addresses of these sports teams are in the almanac.

Name
the Positions
on the
Baseball Field

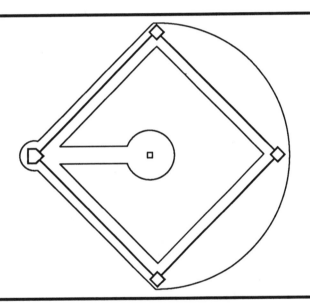

For the correct
answers,
look in books about
baseball or the
encyclopedia.

BASEBALL

WHICH TEAM DO YOU FAVOR?

National League

Atlanta Braves	Chicago Cubs
Cincinnati Reds	Colorado Rockies
Florida Marlins	Houston Astros
Los Angeles Dodgers	Montreal Expos
New York Mets	Philadelphia Phillies
Pittsburgh Pirates	St. Louis Cardinals
San Diego Padres	San Francisco Giants

American League

Baltimore Orioles	Boston Red Sox
California Angels	Chicago White Sox
Cleveland Indians	Detroit Tigers
Kansas City Royals	Milwaukee Brewers
Minnesota Twins	New York Yankees
Oakland A's	Seattle Mariners
Texas Rangers	Toronto Blue Jays

Look for sports books in the card or automated catalog in your library. Write to your favorite team. The address may be found in the almanac.

Football Signals

What is the official saying about these football plays?

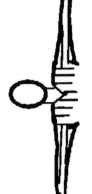

Find out more about the game by browsing in the Dewey Decimal Classification System section 796.332.

The Football Field

Find the goal posts and the kick-off yard line for each team.

10	20	30	40	50	40	30	20	10
10	20	30	40	50	40	30	20	10

Use the automated or card catalog to find more books and materials about FOOTBALL.

NATIONAL FOOTBALL LEAGUE

In which League do these teams play, American or National?
Clue: Use an almanac.

ATLANTA FALCONS
BUFFALO BILLS
CAROLINA PANTHERS
CHICAGO BEARS
CINCINNATI BENGALS
CLEVELAND BROWNS
DALLAS COWBOYS
DENVER BRONCOS
DETROIT LIONS
GREEN BAY PACKERS
HOUSTON OILERS
INDIANAPOLIS COLTS
JACKSONVILLE JAGUARS
KANSAS CITY CHIEFS
LOS ANGELES RAIDERS
LOS ANGELES RAMS
MIAMI DOLPHINS
MINNESOTA VIKINGS
NEW ENGLAND PATRIOTS
NEW ORLEANS SAINTS
NEW YORK GIANTS
NEW YORK JETS
PHILADELPHIA EAGLES
PHOENIX CARDINALS
PITTSBURGH STEELERS
SAN DIEGO CHARGERS
SAN FRANCISCO 49ERS
SEATTLE SEAHAWKS
TAMPA BAY BUCCANEERS
WASHINGTON REDSKINS

50

MORSE CODE

Morse code was used to send radio and telegraph messages. Each dot is made with a quick press and release on the telegraph sender. The short dash is twice as long as the dot and the long dash is four times as long as the dot. To make a space between letters when sent, the sender allows a time equal to three dots.

Can you send a message using the code shown?

Alphabet

A	• —	N	— •
B	— • • •	O	— — —
C	— • — •	P	• — — •
D	— • •	Q	— — • —
E	•	R	• — •
F	• • — •	S	• • •
G	— — •	T	—
H	• • • •	U	• • —
I	• •	V	• • • —
J	• — — —	W	• — —
K	— • —	X	— • • —
L	• — • •	Y	— • — —
M	— —	Z	— — • •

Numerals

1	• — — — —	6	— • • • •
2	• • — — —	7	— — • • •
3	• • • — —	8	— — — • •
4	• • • • —	9	— — — — •
5	• • • • •	0	— — — — —

Punctuation & Symbols

, (comma)	• — • — • —
. (period)	• — • — • —
; (semicolon)	— • — • — •
? (question mark)	• • — — • •
& (and)	• — • • •
$ (dollar)	• • • — • • —

If you want to know more about the code or the inventor, check encyclopedias and reference sources for MORSE, SAMUEL F.; TELEGRAPH; and TELETYPEWRITER.

International Alphabet Flags

Thirty-six flags are used in the International Flag Code. Flags are clipped together for messages.

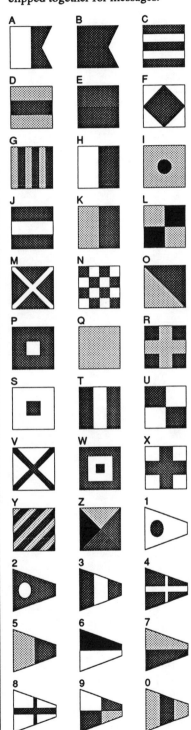

Look in an encyclopedia or book about codes to find out how you might send a message from one ship to another.

BRAILLE

The Braille alphabet is a set of upraised dots punched in thick paper to represent the letters of the alphabet and certain words. See the patterns below. Find copies of books in Braille and feel the writing or read more about the inventor of the system.

A B C D

E F G H

I J K L

M N O P

Q R S T

U V W X

Y Z and for

of the with

Language of the Fan

The use of fans in past ages came to have meaning. This figure is passing on a message. Can you guess what it is? How do we send nonverbal messages today?

Other messages using the fan:

Closing it.
I wish to speak to you.

Twirling in the left hand.
I wish to be rid of you.

Twirling in the right hand.
I love someone else.

Drawing it across the eyes.
I am sorry.

Drawing it across the cheek.
I love you.

Drawing it through the hand.
I hate you.

Handle to lips.
Kiss me.

Dropping.
We are friends.

Read more about the seventeenth, eighteenth, and nineteenth centuries when fans were part of the fashion.

Sign Language

The American manual alphabet is one kind of sign language used by deaf and hearing-impaired. Can you spell your name?

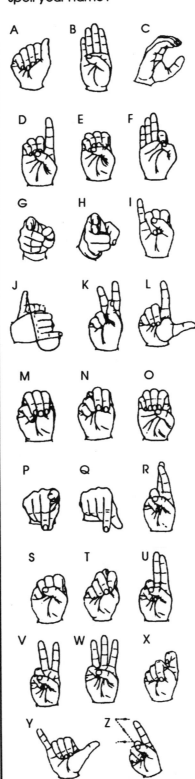

Look for books and materials in the library media center.

Saying Thank You

There are many ways to say thanks. Which language is represented in each of these examples?

Thank you

Gracias

Arigato gozaimasu

Merci beaucoup

Danke schön

To-dá

Bal'shóye spasíba

Syèsye nî

Dziekuje

Answers: English; Spanish; Japanese; French; German; Hebrew; Russian; Chinese; Polish

ALPHABETS

Alphabets of important languages are shown to the right. What do you know about each?

Look for clues in an encyclopedia.

Greek	ΑΒΓ ΔΕΖΗΘΙΚΛΑΜΝΞΟΠΡΣΤΥΦΧΨ Ω
Russian	АБВГДЕЁЖЗИЙКЛМНОПРСТУФХЦЧШЩЬЫЬЭЮЯ
Hindi	अ आ इ ई उ ऊ ऋ ऌ ए ऐ ओ औ क ख ग घ ङ च छ ज झ ञ ट ठ ड ढ ण त थ द ध न प फ ब भ म य र ल व श ष स ह
Arabic	ا ب ت ث ج ح خ د ذ ر ز س ش ص ض ط ظ ع غ ف ق ك ل م ن ه و ي
Gaelic	Abcꝺeꝼ5hilmnopꞃꞃꞇu

©Carolyn S. Brodie, Debra Goodrich, Paula K. Montgomery

Each of these phrases mean the same thing. Are any familiar?

GREEK
HΣYXIA ΠAPAKAΠ

CHINESE
請安靜

ITALIAN
silenzio per favore

YIDDISH
שטיל בײַ זיך שטיל

ARABIC
سكوت من فضلك

FRENCH
silence, s'il vous plait

PANJABI
ਕਿਰਪਾ ਕਰਕੇ ਚੁੱਪ ਰਹੋ

VIETNAMESE
xin giữ im lặng

RUSSIAN
Спокойно, пожалуйста

SPANISH
silencio por favor

Quiet please.

©Carolyn S. Brodie, Debra Goodrich, Paula K. Montgomery

How to Say "I Love You" in Different Languages

AFRIKAANS
Ek is lief vir jou or
Ek het jou liefe
♥

ARABIC
Ana Behibak (to a male) or
Ana Behibek (to a female)
♥

BENGALI
Ami tomAy bhAlobAshi
♥

FRENCH
Je t'aime
♥

GERMAN
Ich liebe Dich
♥

HINDI
Mae tumko peyar kia
♥

JAPANESE
Kimi o ai shiteru
♥

MALAY-INDONESIAN
Sayah Chantikan Awah or
Aku sayang enkow
♥

MANDARIN
Wo ai ni
♥

NAVAHO
Ayor anosh'ni
♥

PORTUGUESE
Eu te amo
♥

RUSSIAN
Ya lyublyu tebya or
Ya vas lyublyu
♥

SPANISH
Te quiero
♥

SWAHILI
Nakupenda
♥

For ways of saying other phrases, look for language books in your library.

©Carolyn S. Brodie, Debra Goodrich, Paula K. Montgomery

Preparing a Research Display

Select a title that grabs attention.

Select and use colors for the background that complement or contrast.

Decide on the graphics and illustrations that will enhance the display and explain the problem and solution.

Place material at eye level for ease of reading and viewing.

Use free standing panels if available made of strong cardboard, plywood, or particleboard that have been properly connected.

Organize material in a logical sequence or order.

Identify other materials that should be displayed in front of the panels.

For more information, find art books in the library.

Steps for Researching an Historical Problem

Identify the problem in history.

Outline the problem.

Identify the kinds of materials that might be useful for finding the answer.

Collect the materials and skim them.

Take notes and document the sources.

Organize the notes.

Make inferences from notes.

Write a draft related to the problem.

Correct the draft and finish the paper.

Investigate the resources in the library that might be useful for finding out about historical problems.

Steps for Researching a Science Problem

- Identify the Problem or Question
- Prepare a Hypothesis
- Develop a Procedure
- Collect Materials
- Collect Data
- Draw Conclusions

Use the encyclopedia to think of topics and questions that might be worth researching.

Animal Groups

What would you call a group of these animals?

Match the words that are used for grouping with the correct animal group.

bed	bears
brace	bees
brood	cats
clutter	cattle
colony	chickens
company	crows
crush	ducks
flock	elk
gang	foxes
herd	hawks
kettle	kangaroos
knot	kittens
leap	leopards
litter	lions
murder	locusts
nest	nightingales
pack	oysters or clams
plague	parrots
pod	ponies
pride	rabbits
skulk	rhinoceroses
sloth	sheep
string	termites, bees, or ants
swarm	toads
troop	whales or seals
watch	wolves

Answers: school of fish; bed of oysters or clams; brace of ducks; brood of chickens; clutter of cats; colony of termites, bees, or ants; company of parrots; crush of rhinoceroses; flock of sheep; gang of elk; herd of cattle; kettle of hawks; knot of toads; litter of kittens; leap of leopards; murder of crows; nest of rabbits; pack of wolves; plague of locusts; pod of whales or seals; pride of lions; skulk of foxes; sloth of bears; string of ponies; swarm of bees; troop of kangaroos; watch of nightingales

©Carolyn S. Brodie, Debra Goodrich, Paula K. Montgomery

Animal Classifications

Animals are classified by their characteristics. Into what classifications do these animals fit? What makes each animal different?

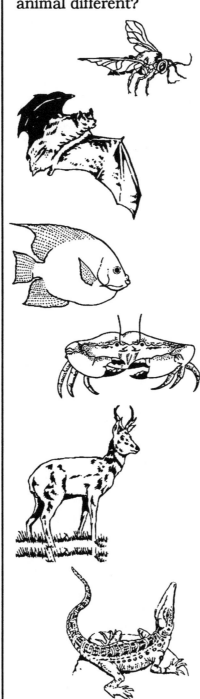

Find books about animals in the library to help in your quest.

©Carolyn S. Brodie, Debra Goodrich, Paula K. Montgomery

Fantasy Animals

Some animals that we read about are not real. We call them fantasy or imaginary creatures. Can you identify these?

You will encounter some of these creatures in mythology or in fantasy fiction books. Use the card or automated catalog to find something of interest to read.

©Carolyn S. Brodie, Debra Goodrich, Paula K. Montgomery

Invertebrates

Which animal is not an invertebrate?

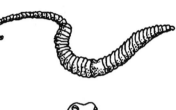

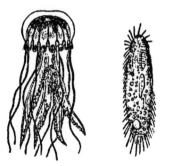

If you don't know what an invertebrate is, look for the word in the dictionary.

Answer: frog

Vertebrates

What kind of vertebrate is each of these animals? Amphibian; Reptile; Fish; Bird, or Mammal? Can you think of an example of other kinds of vertebrates?

Find out more about vertebrates in the Dewey Decimal Classification System section 500 of the library.

Insects

Insects abound in the world. What kind of insect is this?

Use insect identification guide books to help identify these.

56

Fishes

Fish are believed to have been in existence for hundreds of thousands of years. There are many kinds that differ in the way they obtain food and the way they are structured.

Each of these fish is from a different class. What can you find out about the environment of each fish?

Jawless Fishes: lampreys
Cartilaginous Fishes: sharks
Fleshy-Finned Fishes: lungfishes
Ray-Finned Fishes: sturgeons
Bonefish
Eels
Herrings
Bony Tongues: butterfly fish
Salmon
Catfishes
Toadfishes
Flying Fish
Sea Horses
Rockfish
Tuna
Flatfishes: flounder
Box Fishes

Clue: Look for guide books and identification books showing fish in the library.

Amphibians

Where do these animals begin their lives?

Find out more about amphibians by looking for videotapes about them. Find the workd AMPHIBIAN in the card or automated catalog for help in your library.

Answer: water

REPTILES

What do these animals have in common?

These animals belong to the animal class of reptiles, vertebrates with internal fertilization and scaly bodies.

You can find more information about reptiles in the encyclopedia.

MAMMALS

Mammals are animals with backbones and hair that nurse their young with milk from glands in the mother. There are two subclasses of mammals: Prototheria and Theria. An example is given in parentheses. What is your favorite mammal?

Prototheria - Ornithodelphia - Monotremata (platypus)

Theria - Metatheria - Marsupialia (kangaroo)

Theria - Eutheria - Insectivora (mole)

Theria - Eutheria - Dermoptera (flying lemur)

Theria - Eutheria - Chiroptera (bat)

Theria - Eutheria - Primates (chimpanzee)

Theria - Eutheria - Edentata (armadillo)

Theria - Eutheria - Pholidota (pangolin)

Theria - Eutheria - Tubulidentata (aardvark)

Theria - Eutheria - Lagomorpha (rabbit)

Theria - Eutheria - Rodentia (mouse)

Theria - Eutheria - Mysticeti (blue whale)

Theria - Eutheria - Odontoceti (dolphin)

Theria - Eutheria - Carnivora (bear)

Theria - Eutheria - Proboscidea (elephant)

Theria - Eutheria - Hyracoidea (hyrax)

Theria - Eutheria - Sirenia (manatee)

Theria - Eutheria - Perissodactyla (horse)

Theria - Eutheria - Artiodactyla (giraffe)

Animal Babies

What are these animal babies called?

Find picture books about these baby animals in your library.

Answers:
Chick, Lamb, Colt, Puppy, Kitten

Taking Care of Your Pet

Check yourself. Are you taking good care of your pet?

✓ Does your pet have a nutritious diet?

✓ Are food dishes clean?

✓ Do you provide fresh clean water for your pet?

✓ Does your pet stay in an adequate house or place to stay?

✓ Do your pets have what they need to keep clean?

✓ Do you help your pet prevent illness with necessary trips to a veterinarian or with innoculations, if required?

You can find out more about good pet care in books and other materials in the library.

MAKING THINGS FROM NATURE

We make many things from natural products. Just for fun, what can you make from a nut?

Miss Hickory, a book by Carolyn Sherwin Bailey, is about a doll with a head made of a nut.

What other natural objects can be used to make things?

Look for other craft books in the card or automated catalog under terms such as NATURE STUDY–ACTIVITIES or CRAFTS–NATURE.

Types of Trees

There are six main groups of trees. Look at the examples. Can you think of others that fit into the group?

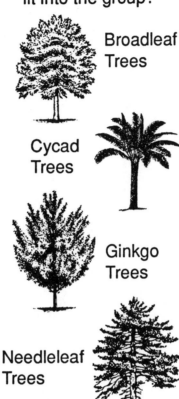

Broadleaf Trees

Cycad Trees

Ginkgo Trees

Needleleaf Trees

Palms

Tree Ferns

Clue: Look for tree identification books and videotapes for ideas and more information.

Parts of a Flower

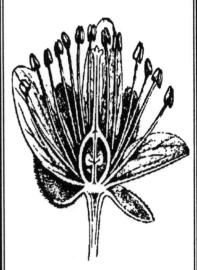

Can you locate these parts of the flower?

Petals
Stem
Stamen
Pistil

Use books and videotapes about plants and flowers to find the answers.

Symbolic Meanings of Trees

Trees have been symbolic of different ideas. Which ones have you seen?

Balsam
  Impatience
Chestnut
  Render Me
  Justice
Cypress
  Death and
  Eternal Sorrow
Dogwood
  Durability
Elm
  Dignity
Hemlock
  You Will Cause
  My Death
Maple
  Reserve
Oak
  Hospitality
Palm
  Victory
Pine
  Pity
Walnut
  Intellect
White Oak
  Independence

For other tree meanings, look for books about symbols and plants.

©Carolyn S. Brodie, Debra Goodrich, Paula K. Montgomery

Meanings of Flowers

If someone gave you this flower, what might it mean?

Buttercup
Childishness
Cherry Tree Blossom
Spiritual Beauty
Crocus
Cheerfulness
Daisy
Innocence
Forget-Me-Not
True Love
Hibiscus
Delicate Beauty
Honeysuckle
Bond of Love
Laurel
Glory
Narcissus
Egotism
Peony
Bashful Shame
Sweet Violet
Modesty
White Lily
Purity and Modesty

For other flower meanings, look for books about symbols and plants.

©Carolyn S. Brodie, Debra Goodrich, Paula K. Montgomery

Parts of a Leaf

Leaves are made up of two main parts: blade and leafstalk.

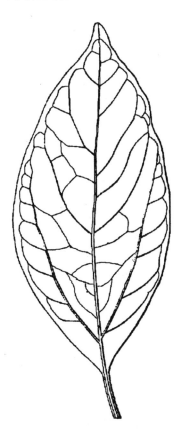

Leaves differ in the kind of edges they have. What are those kinds?

Clue: Find LEAF in an encyclopedia or science encyclopedia or dictionary.

Answer: smooth-edged, toothed, and lobed leaf blade

Measuring Temperature

What is your temperature in Celius when it is 98.6° Fahrenheit?

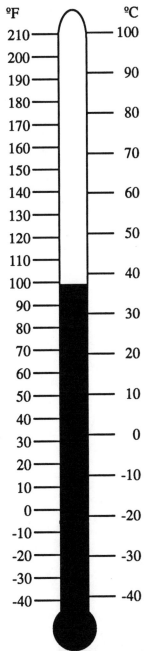

°F	°C
210	100
200	90
190	90
180	80
170	80
160	70
150	
140	60
130	
120	50
110	40
100	
90	30
80	
70	20
60	
50	10
40	
30	0
20	
10	-10
0	-20
-10	
-20	-30
-30	-40
-40	

Check science dictionaries and encyclopedias for information about the difference between the two scales for measuring temperature.

Answer: 37°

Barometer Reading

What is barometric pressure?

How does the barometer give clues about the weather? Low or high pressure?

When it goes down, there might be a storm.

When it goes up, the weather may be dry.

Find books about weather in the library.

Types of Precipitation

Can you identify these meteorological symbols of precipitation?

Find books about weather in Dewey Decimal Classification System section 551.57.

Answer: Rain; Hail; Sleet; Snow

61

Clouds

Which clouds might bring rain or snow?

Cirrus
Cirrocumulus
Cirrostratus
Altostratus
Stratocumulus
Stratus
Nimbostratus
Cumulus
Cumulonimbus

Clue:
Search encyclopedias and weather reference books for information about the ten major types of clouds.

Answer: altostratus, cirrocumulus, stratus, nimbostratus, stratocumulus, cumulonimbus

©Carolyn S. Brodie, Debra Goodrich, Paula K. Montgomery

WEATHER TERMS

We have terms to describe certain kinds of weather conditions.

HUMIDITY
a measure of the amount of water vapor in the air

PRECIPITATION
moisture that falls from the air in the form of hail, rain, snow, sleet, snow

TEMPERATURE
the amount or degree of heat in the air

WIND
movement of the air

Look for other weather terms in the glossaries of books about weather.

©Carolyn S. Brodie, Debra Goodrich, Paula K. Montgomery

Natural Disasters
There have been many natural disasters. Are these the worst that have been recorded in history?

Fires
On October 8, 1871, in Peshtigo, Wisconsin, a forest fire killed over 1,200 people and burned more than 2 billion trees.

Floods
A flood of the Huang He River in China killed an estimated 3,700,000 people.

Earthquakes
An earthquake measured 8.7 on the Richter Scale on August 15, 1950, in Assam, India.

Storms
Hurricane Andrew, which hit South Florida, was the most costly hurricane in U.S. history.

Clue: Use an almanac or *The Guinness Book of World Records* for help.

©Carolyn S. Brodie, Debra Goodrich, Paula K. Montgomery

Dinosaurs in the Triassic Period

The Mesozoic Era began 240 million years ago. It can be classified into three time periods. The oldest period was called the Triassic Period.

Can you identify these dinosaurs from the Triassic Period?

Look for information about these and other dinosaurs in books and videotapes in the library.

Plateosaurus; Compsognathus; Teratosaurus; Procompsognathus; Hesperosuchus

©Carolyn S. Brodie, Debra Goodrich, Paula K. Montgomery

Dinosaurs in the Jurassic Period

The Mesozoic Era began 240 million years ago. It can be classified into three time periods. The next to the oldest period within this era was called the Jurassic Period.

Can you identify these dinosaurs from the Jurassic Period?

Look for information about these and other dinosaurs in books and videotapes in the library.

Allosaurus; Brachiosaurus; Camarasaurus; Diplodocus; Stegosaurus

©Carolyn S. Brodie, Debra Goodrich, Paula K. Montgomery

Dinosaurs in the Cretaceous Period

The Mesozoic Era began 240 million years ago. It can be classified into three time periods. The youngest period in the era was called the Cretaceous Period.

Can you identify these dinosaurs from the Cretaceous Period?

Look for information about these and other dinosaurs in books and videotapes in the library.

Deinonychus; Parasaurolophus; Spinosaurus; Triceratops; Tyrannosaurus Rex

©Carolyn S. Brodie, Debra Goodrich, Paula K. Montgomery

GEOLOGIC FORMATIONS

Three major kinds of rocks may be found on the earth's surface.

Which of the names of these rocks fits in the category? Look at the names and draw a line to the kind of rock you think it is.

sandstone
granite
lava
limestone
marble

Metamorphic

Igneous

Sedimentary

Clue: Look for rock and mineral identification guides in your library.

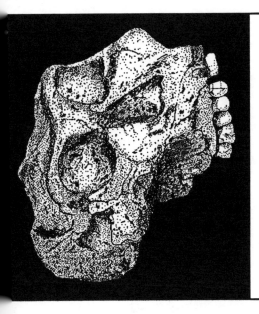

Prehistoric Man

Remains of these species have been found. When do archaeologists believe that the species lived?

Australopithecus

Homo Habilis

Homo Erectus

Neanderthal

Homo Sapiens

Make your best guess and then look them up in an encyclopedia under terms such as prehistoric life.

PREHISTORIC TIME LINE

Millions of Years Ago	ERA and Period	Events
4600	PRECAMBRIAN Precambrian	Formation of the Earth's crust; algae
	(Precambrian era lasted over four billion years.)	
600 +	PALAEOZOIC Cambrian	Marine animals with mineralized shells: trilobites, echinoderms, brachiopods, molluscs, primitive graptolites
500 +	Ordovician	Graptolites dominant; also trilobites, brachiopods, bryozoans, gastropods, bivalves, echinoids, crinoids, cephalopods, and corals
450 +	Silurian	Barchiopods, crinoids, corals; primitive fish
400 +	Devonian (395)	Corals, brachiopods, ammonoids, crinoids; fishes and early land plants
350 +	Carboniferous (345)	Foraminiferans, corals, bryozoans, brachiopods, blastoids; seed ferns, lycopsids, and other plants; amphibians
300 +	Permian	Amphibians and reptiles; gymnosperms dominant plants
250 +	MESOZOIC Triassic	Molluscs dominant invertebrates; reptiles dominant: turtles, dinosaurs, ichthyosaurs
	Jurassic	Ferns, cycads, ginkgos, rushes, conifers; ammonites and other invertebrates; pterosaurs, Archaeopteryx appears
150 +	Cretaceous (136)	Angiosperm plants; Mesozoic reptiles peak
100 +	CENOZOIC Tertiary (65)	Modern animals, shrubs, grasses, and other flowering plants
Present +	Quarternary (1.8)	

Can you decide which appeared to evolve first, the trilobite or the turtle? Look for clues on the chart or find books about prehistoric life in your library.

Can You Name the Planets?

Clue: You can find books about the solar system in Dewey Decimal Classification System section 523.2 or 523.4

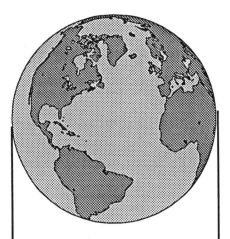

FACTS ABOUT THE EARTH

The earth is the fifth largest planet in the solar system.

•

The earth is about 4.55 billion years old.

•

The diameter of the earth at the equator is 7,926 miles.

•

The surface of the earth is covered with 71% water and 29% land.

•

What other facts can you collect about the earth by using encyclopedias, reference books, and audiovisual materials?

©Carolyn S. Brodie, Debra Goodrich, Paula K. Montgomery

SUN STATISTICS

How many characteristics and statistics can you add to this list about the sun?

Diameter at equator: 1,392,000 km.

Mean Distance from Earth: 149,000,000 km. or 92,960,000 mi.

Gravity: _____

Surface Temperature: 6000° C

Core Temperature:
_____

Number of Spins on Axis: _____

Orbits Galaxy: 225 million years

Clues: Browse for information in the Dewey Decimal Classification System number 523.7 section.

©Carolyn S. Brodie, Debra Goodrich, Paula K. Montgomery

Moon Statistics

Are these statements about the moon correct?

The moon is the earth's closest major neighbor in the solar system.

The moon is a natural satellite that circles the earth once every 28 days.

The moon travels in an elliptical orbit around the earth.

The moon affects the earth's gravity pulling the water in oceans away from the earth.

There is no sound on the moon because there is no atmosphere.

Clue: Browse in the Dewey Decimal Classification number 523.3 section for information about the moon.

©Carolyn S. Brodie, Debra Goodrich, Paula K. Montgomery

The Universe

Galaxies are aggregates stars, gas, and dust clustered together and separated by a large empty space.

Our galaxy is called the

_____.

It is about

_____

light years in diameter.

It is about

_____

light years in thickness.

Scientists believe it is a spiral

_____.

The nearest spiral galaxy to the Milky Way is

_____.

Clues: Find more information about galaxies in science encyclopedias.

Answer: Milky Way; 100,000; 10,000; nebula; Andromeda

©Carolyn S. Brodie, Debra Goodrich, Paula K. Montgomery

On each of the following dates, a special space flight event began. Can you find out what it was? Why was the flight special? What are other important dates?

April 12, 1961

April 5, 1961

June 16, 1963

July 16, 1969

August 20, 1975

September 5, 1977

December 21, 1987

Clue: Look for SPACE FLIGHT in the card or automated catalog to find books and audiovisual materials about these events.

Answer: First manned orbital flight; First American in space; First woman in space; First lunar landing; Viking I landed on Mars; Voyager I passed Jupiter and showed rings; Set space endurance record

©Carolyn S. Brodie, Debra Goodrich, Paula K. Montgomery

FAMOUS FATHERS

Find out more about these men who are considered to be fathers. What did they do?

FATHER OF HIS COUNTRY
George Washington

FATHER OF MEDICINE
Hippocrates

FATHER OF THE SYMPHONY
Franz Joseph Haydn

FATHER OF HISTORY
Herodutus

Father's Day is celebrated the third Sunday in June.

Clue: Use encyclopedias to find the names of the men.

©Carolyn S. Brodie, Debra Goodrich, Paula K. Montgomery

Famous Mothers

What was special about these mothers?

Whistler's Mother

Demeter

Mother Goose

Old Mother Hubbard

Mother's Day is celebrated the second Sunday in May.

Clue: These names may be found in encyclopedias or reference books about characters in literature.

©Carolyn S. Brodie, Debra Goodrich, Paula K. Montgomery

Famous Brothers and Sisters

These brothers and sisters are well known in history or literature. Find out what you can about them in the library.

Marx Brothers:
Arthur (Harpo),
Herbert (Zeppo),
Julius (Groucho),
Leonard (Chico), and
Milton (Gummo)

Andrew Sisters

Jacob and Esau

Romulus and Remus

Cain and Abel

Apollo and Artemis (Diana)

Beezus and Ramona

Hansel and Gretel

Little Women

Mary, Laura, Carrie, and Grace Ingalls

©Carolyn S. Brodie, Debra Goodrich, Paula K. Montgomery

The Nobel Prize

Nobel Prizes are awarded under the will of Alfred Bernhard Nobel, Swedish chemist and engineer. The annual interest is divided among the persons who have been selected as making the most outstanding contribution in fields of physics, chemistry, physiology or medicine, literature, peace, and economic sciences.

About how much money is earned yearly in interest for the prize?

Clue: Use almanacs for basic information and look for current periodical indexes to locate articles about the most recent award ceremonies.

NOBEL PRIZE WINNERS

Can you find the answers to these?

When did Isaac Bashevis Singer win the prize for literature?

For what did the Dalai Lama win a Nobel prize?

Who won the physics award for discovering the neutron?

For what did Willard F. Libby win the 1960 chemistry award?

Who won the award for medicine in 1945 and for what?

Clue: Almanacs are an excellent source for finding information about Nobel Prize winners.

Answer: 1978; Peace: James Chadwick; atomic time clock; Sir Alexander Fleming, Ernst Boris Chain, and Sir Howard Florey for the discovery of penicillin

ACADEMY AWARDS

Find the answers to these questions.

What was the name of the best picture in 1943?

Whoopi Goldberg won an Oscar in what year for what role in the movie, *Ghost*?

What was the name of the best picture in 1968 that was based on a book by Charles Dickens?

Charlton Heston won best actor in 1959 in what movie set in Rome?

What movie made about the life of a famous person won the award in 1982?

What actor won an award for *To Kill a Mockingbird*?

Clue: Find academy awards in the index of an almanac to identify the missing winners.

Answers: *Casablanca*; Supporting Actress in 1990; *Oliver!*; *Ben Hur*; *Gandhi*; Gregory Peck

Revolutionary War

What did these individuals do during the Revolutionary War?

George Washington
John Hancock
John Adams
Thomas Jefferson
Patrick Henry
Thomas Paine
Deborah Sampson
Marquis de Lafayette
Crispus Attucks

Clue: Find history materials in the Dewey Decimal Classification System number 973.3 or use biographies about the individuals.

Revolutionary War

What was the significance of each of these events?

Sugar Act—1764
Stamp Act—1765
Boston Massacre—1770
Boston Tea Party—1773
First Continental Congress—1774
Battle of Lexington and Concord—1775
Declaration of Independence—1776
Washington defeats Hessians at Trenton—1776-1777
Burgoyne surrenders to Gates at Saratoga—1777
France recognizes America's Independence—1778
British capture Savannah—1778
Cornwallis surrenders at Yorktown, Virginia—1781
Peace of Paris—1783

Clue: Use history sources in the library. Look for materials on United States—History—Revolutionary War

Civil War

What were the views of these individuals who lived during the Civil War?

Clara Barton
Anna Ella Carroll
Jefferson Davis
Frederick Douglass
Ulysses S. Grant
Robert E. Lee
Abraham Lincoln
William Tecumseh Sherman

Clue: Find biographies and biographical information about these and other individuals living during this time in the library.

Civil War

These are important events that occurred during the Civil War. Are they listed in correct chronological order? If not, rearrange them correctly.

Emancipation Proclamation

Confederate victory at Second Battle of Bull Run

General Sherman occupies Savannah

Monitor and Merrimac duel at Hampton Roads

Union stopped Confederates at Vicksburg

Confederates take Fort Sumter

Battle of Chancellorsville, Virginia

Lee stopped at Gettysburg

Confederacy surrenders at Appomattox

Abraham Lincoln elected President of the United States

Battle at Antietam

Lincoln's Gettysburg Address

Ulysses Grant made Commander of Union Army

Clue: Use materials about the Civil War found in your library.

World War I

Who were the leaders of the countries involved in the war?

CENTRAL POWERS
Germany
Austria-Hungary
Turkey

ALLIES
France
Great Britain
Russia
Italy
Japan
United States

World War I

Mark places on this map that were the sites of important events during World War I.

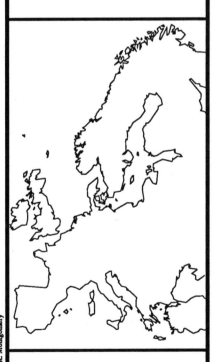

Clue: Look in the automated or card catalog for books about this war.

World War II

Place these events in chronological order.

Japan attacks Pearl Harbor

U.S. drops Atomic Bomb on Hiroshima

German Invasion of Poland

Casablanca Conference

D-Day

Germans enter Paris

Yalta Agreement

Hilter attacks Russia

For information about these and other events, locate videotapes and books in the library.

Answers: German Invasion of Poland (1939); Germans enter Paris (1940); Hilter attacks Russia (June 22, 1941); Japan attacks Pearl Harbor (Dec. 7, 1941); Casablanca Conference (January 14, 1943); D-Day (June 6, 1944); Yalta Conference (February 11, 1945); Hiroshima Atomic Bomb Attack (August 6, 1945).

©Carolyn S. Brodie, Debra Goodrich, Paula K. Montgomery

World War II

What was the role of these individuals during World War II?

Winston Churchill
Harry S. Truman
Joseph Stalin
Benito Mussolini
Adolf Hitler
Franklin D. Roosevelt
Emperor Hirohito

Clue: Use encyclopedias and biographical reference sources in the library.

©Carolyn S. Brodie, Debra Goodrich, Paula K. Montgomery

✌ Vietnam Conflict ✌

Draw a line between the correct dates and the events.

Four students killed by National Guard at Kent State	March 13, 1954
North Vietnamese Army captures Saigon	July 8, 1959
Vietminh defeat French	January 2, 1963
President Nixon authorizes renewed bombing of North Vietnam	August 1, 1964
Cease-fire agreement between U.S, North and South Vietnam signed	February 24, 1965
	March 8, 1965
Two Marine battalions land at Da Nang	
	January 31, 1968
Two Americans killed at Bien Hoa	
Vietcong defeat Army of the Republic of Vietnam	March 18, 1969
North Vietnamese attack U.S. Destroyer *Maddox*	May 4, 1970
U.S. begins Operation Rolling Thunder	April 15, 1972
Tet Offensive begins	January 27, 1973
Nixon begins secret bombing on Ho ChiMinh Trail	April 30, 1975

Clue: Use the encyclopedia and periodicals for information that might help complete this matching activity.

©Carolyn S. Brodie, Debra Goodrich, Paula K. Montgomery

Finding Locations Using a Map Grid

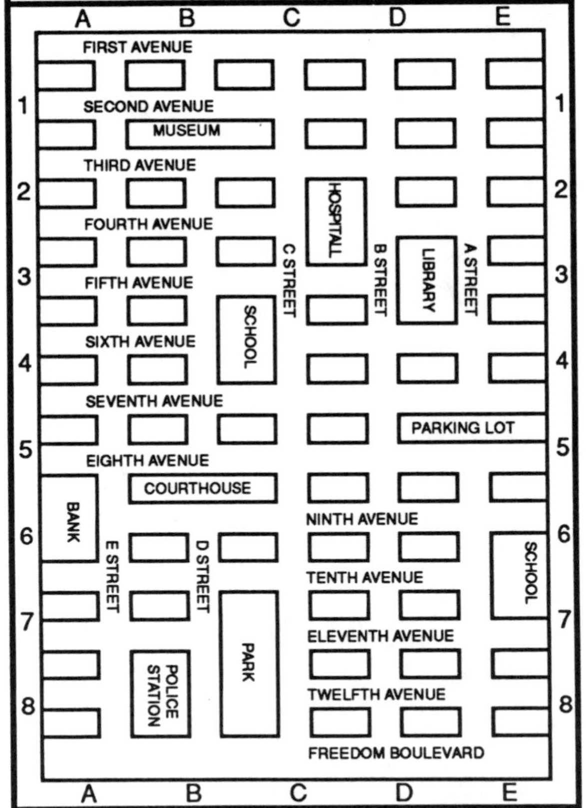

The map grid shows streets (A STREET, B STREET, C STREET, D STREET, E STREET) and avenues (FIRST AVENUE, SECOND AVENUE, THIRD AVENUE, FOURTH AVENUE, FIFTH AVENUE, SIXTH AVENUE, SEVENTH AVENUE, EIGHTH AVENUE, NINTH AVENUE, TENTH AVENUE, ELEVENTH AVENUE, TWELFTH AVENUE, FREEDOM BOULEVARD). Locations include: LIBRARY, MUSEUM, HOSPITAL, SCHOOL, PARKING LOT, SCHOOL, COURTHOUSE, PARK, POLICE STATION, BANK.

Grid columns labeled A, B, C, D, E across top and bottom; rows labeled 1–8 at left and right.

Some maps have grids to help locate a place. Letters, usually beginning with "A," run across the top and bottom of the map. Numbers, usually beginning with "1," run on the right and left. To locate a place on the map, read the letter and number signifying the location. Find the area where a letter and number intersect or cross each other. The place for which you are searching will be in that vicinity.

©Carolyn S. Brodie, Debra Goodrich, Paula K. Montgomery

Reading Map Symbols

Match the symbols to the meanings.

Railroad

Capital

Camp Site

Hospital

Scale

Picnic Area

Airport

Road

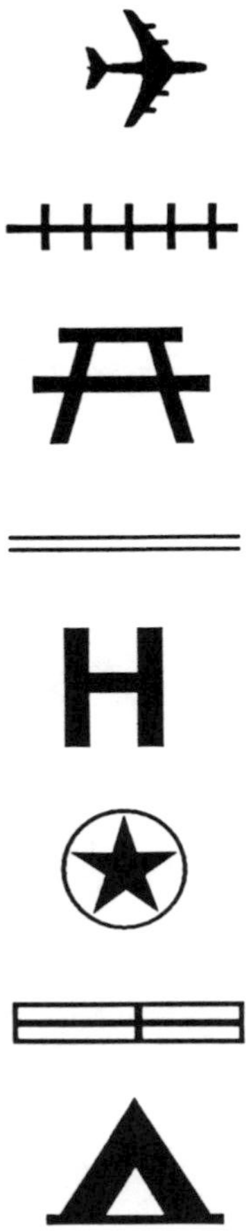

For more information about maps and map reading, look for books in your library.

©Carolyn S. Brodie, Debra Goodrich, Paula K. Montgomery

ROAD SIGN SYMBOLS

What do these road signs mean?

Answers: Stop; Yield; School Zone; Railway Crossing; Men Working

©Carolyn S. Brodie, Debra Goodrich, Paula K. Montgomery

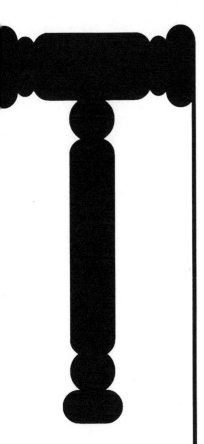

U.S. Supreme Court

Name the members of the U.S. Supreme Court.
How many are there?

Clue: Use an almanac for current names.

U.S. Congress

Fill-in the blanks.

The legislative branch of the United States government is made of the Congress, which consists of the

_____

and

_____.

Each state has representation in the U.S. Congress. How many does your state have in each branch of Congress? What are their names? How can you contact them?

Answers: Use the almanac, telephone directory, *Official Congressional Directory*, *Congressional Staff Directory*, or *U.S. Government Manual* for information.

Executive Branch of the U.S. Government

Who is responsible for the executive branch of the government?

What agencies and cabinet members help the current executive carry out the functions of the job?

Clue: Look in an encyclopedia for basic information and an almanac for names of individuals.

Uncle Sam

Uncle Sam is a popular nickname and symbol for the government of the United States. It was first used during the War of 1812. Find the origin of Uncle Sam's name and the reason for it.

Use encyclopedias and government reference sources to learn the story.

Answer: Samuel Wilson, owner of a meatpacking plant in Troy, New York.

©Carolyn S. Brodie, Debra Goodrich, Paula K. Montgomery

Statue of Liberty Facts

What do you know about the Statue of Liberty?

From whom was the statue a gift?

Who was the sculptor who created the statue?

How much does the statue weigh overall?

How high does the statute stand from feet to torch?

Use the almanac or encyclopedia to find the answers.

Answers: People of France presented it to the U.S. on July 4, 1884, and dedicated it on October 28, 1886; Frederick Auguste Bartholdi; 225 short tons or 204 metric tons; 151 feet 1 inch (46.05 m)

©Carolyn S. Brodie, Debra Goodrich, Paula K. Montgomery

The New Colossus

Not like the brazen giant of
   Greek fame,
With conquering limbs
   astride from land to land;
Here at our sea-washed, sun
   set gates shall stand
A mighty woman with a
   torch, whose flame
Is the imprisoned lightning,
   and her name
Mother of exiles, From her
   beacon-hand
Glows world-wide welcome;
   her mild eyes command
The air-bridged harbor that
   twin cities frame.
"Keep, ancient lands, your
   storied pomp!" cries she
With silent lips. "Give me
   your tired, your poor,
Your huddled masses yearn-
   ing to breathe free,
The wretched refuse of your
   teeming shore.
Send these, the homeless,
   tempest-tost to me.
I lift my lamp beside the
   golden door!"
        —Emma Lazarus

Who was Emma Lazarus?

Clue: Look in encyclopedias and biographical reference books in the library.

©Carolyn S. Brodie, Debra Goodrich, Paula K. Montgomery

The Liberty Bell

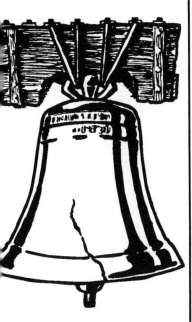

When did the Liberty Bell crack?

Clue: Look for information in encyclopedias and almanacs.

Preamble to the U.S. Constitution

We the people of the United States, in Order to form a more perfect Union, establish Justice, insure domestic Tranquility, provide for the common defence, promote the general Welfare, and secure the Blessings of Liberty to ourselves and our Posterity do ordain and establish this Constitution for the United States of America.

What does this document guarantee We the People of the United States?

Clue: Use general reference books in the library for a complete copy of the document.

Declaration of Independence

When in the Course of human Events, it becomes necessary for one people to dissolve the political bands which have connected them with another, and to assume among the Powers of the earth, the separate and equal station to which the Laws of Nature and of Nature's God entitle them, a decent respect to the opinions of mankind requires that they should declare the causes which impel them to the separation.

We hold these truths to be self-evident, that all men are created equal, that they are endowed by their Creator with certain unalienable Rights, that among these are Life, Liberty and the Pursuit of Happiness....

What is the history of this document and its signing?

Use reference sources in the library to find a complete copy of the document.

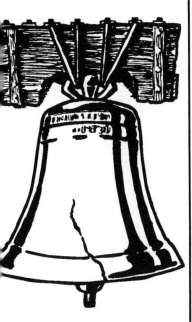

©Carolyn S. Brodie, Debra Goodrich, Paula K. Montgomery

©Carolyn S. Brodie, Debra Goodrich, Paula K. Montgomery

©Carolyn S. Brodie, Debra Goodrich, Paula K. Montgomery

The Great Seal of the United States

The Continental Congress appointed a committee of Benjamin Franklin, John Adams, and Thomas Jefferson to "bring a device for a seal of the United States of America" on July 4, 1776. A design by William Barton was approved by Congress on June 20, 1782.

Where are the designs on the seal commonly seen?

Clue: Examine U.S. paper money.

Displaying the Flag

Federal law requires that the U.S. flag should be displayed from sunrise to sunset. It may displayed after sunset if illuminated.

The U. S. flag is placed above a state flag on the same pole.

When flown with other national flags, fly the U.S. flag on the pole on the far left.

Hang a U.S. flag flat against wall behind a speaker with stars to the viewer's left.

Place the U.S. flag on a pole to the speaker's right.

Hang a U.S. flag vertically in window with canton to the left of a viewer on the outside of the building.

What are other ways in which we show respect for the U.S. flag? Clues: Use encyclopedias or almanacs for correct display of the flag.

Pledge of Allegiance

I pledge allegiance to the flag of the United States of America and to the republic for which it stands, one Nation under God, indivisible, with liberty and justice for all.

Who wrote this pledge?

When and where was it published?

Clue: Look in encyclopedias and almanacs for help.

Answer: Either James B. Upton or Francis Bellamy; September 8, 1892, in *The Youth's Companion.*

The Star-Spangled Banner

Can you fill in the missing words?

Oh! say, can you see, by
    the dawn's early light
What so _____
    we hailed at the
    twilight's last gleaming?
Whose broad _____
    and bright _____,
    thro' the perilous fight,
O'er the ramparts we
    watched were so gal-
    lantly streaming?
And the rockets' red glare,
    the bombs bursting in
    air,
Gave proof through the
    night that our
    _____ was still
    there.
Oh! say, does that
    _____
    banner yet wave
O'er the land of the
    _____ and the
    home of the
    _____?

              Francis Scott Key

Find copies of the music and the
other verses of our national anthem.
Clues: Use an automated or card
catalog for sources.

Answers: proudly; stripes; stars; flag; star-
spangled; free; brave.

Gettysburg Address

Four score and seven years ago our fathers brought forth on this continent, a new nation, conceived in Liberty, and dedicated to the proposition that all men are created equal.

Now we are engaged in a great civil war, testing whether that nation, or any nation so conceived and so dedicated, can long endure. We are met on a great battlefield of that war. We have come to dedicate a portion of that field, as a final resting place for those who here gave their lives that that nation might live. It is altogether fitting and proper that we should do this.

But, in a larger sense, we can not dedicate—we can not consecrate— we can not hallow—this ground. The brave men, living and dead, who struggled here, have consecrated it, far above our poor power to add or detract. The world will little note, nor long remember what we say here, but it can never forget what they did here. It is for us the living, rather, to be dedicated here to the unfinished work which they who fought here have thus far so nobly advanced. It is rather for us to be here dedicated to the great task remaining before us—that from these honored dead we take increased devotion to that cause for which they gave the last full measure of devotion—that we here highly resolve that these dead shall not have died in vain—that this nation, under God, shall have a new birth of freedom—and that government of the people, by the people, for the people, shall not perish from the earth.

On what occasion was this speech
delivered?

Clue: Use reference sources (encyclopedia, almanac, and history books) for
the background of Lincoln's speech.

Answer: November 19, 1863, dedication of
the national cemetery at Gettysburg.

★ Presidents and Dates Served ★

Fill-in the missing dates.

Name	Dates Served
George Washington	1789-1797
John Adams	1797-1801
Thomas Jefferson	1801-
James Madison	-1817
James Monroe	1817-1825
John Quincy Adams	1825-1829
Andrew Jackson	1829-
Martin Van Buren	-1841
William H. Harrison	1841-
John Tyler	-1845
James K. Polk	1845-1849
Zachary Taylor	1849-
Millard Fillmore	-1853
Franklin Pierce	1853-1857
James Buchanan	1857-1861
Abraham Lincoln	1861-1865
Andrew Johnson	1865-
Ulysses S. Grant	-1877
Rutherford B. Hayes	1877-1881
James A. Garfield	1881-
Chester A. Arthur	-1885
Grover Cleveland	1885-1889
Benjamin Harrison	1889-1893
Grover Cleveland	1893-1897
William McKinley	1897-1901
Theodore Roosevelt	1901-1909
William H. Taft	1909-
Woodrow Wilson	-1921
Warren G. Harding	1921-1923
Calvin Coolidge	1923-1929
Herbert C. Hoover	1929-
Franklin D. Roosevelt	-1945
Harry S. Truman	1945-1953
Dwight D. Eisenhower	1953-1961
John F. Kennedy	1961-
Lyndon B. Johnson	-1969
Richard M. Nixon	1969-1974
Gerald R. Ford	1974-1977
Jimmy Carter	1977-1981
Ronald W. Reagan	1981-1989
George H. W. Bush	1989-1993
Bill Clinton	1993-

Answers: Look in a current almanac or
encyclopedia.

©Carolyn S. Brodie, Debra Goodrich, Paula K. Montgomery

Alabama

Capital
Montgomery

Nickname
Heart of Dixie,
Camellia State,
or
Yellowhammer State

Motto
We dare defend our
rights.

Bird
Yellowhammer

Flower
Camellia

Tree
Southern Pine

Song
"Alabama"

If you want more
brief facts, look in
an almanac.

ALASKA

CAPITAL
Juneau

NICKNAME
Land of the Midnight Sun
or
Last Frontier

MOTTO
North to the future.

BIRD
Alaska Willow Ptarmigan
(willow grouse)

FLOWER
Forget-Me-Not

TREE
Sitka Spruce

SONG
"Alaska's Flag"

If you want more
information, use an
encyclopedia.

ARIZONA

Capital
Phoenix

Nickname
Grand Canyon State,
Apache State,
or
Copper State

Motto
God enriches.

Bird
Cactus Wren

Flower
Saguaro Flower

Tree
Paloverde

Song
"Arizona March Song"

If you want more
information, find Dewey
Decimal Classification
number 979.1 on the
library shelves.

Arkansas

Capital
Little Rock

Nickname
Land of
opportunity

Motto
The people rule.

Bird
Mockingbird

Flower
Apple Blossom

Tree
Pine

Song
"Arkansas"

• • •

If you want more
information,
see Kane's *Facts
about the States.*

CALIFORNIA

Capital
Sacramento

Nickname
The Golden State

Motto
Eureka!
(I have found it!)

Bird
California Valley Quail

Flower
Golden Poppy

Tree
California Redwood

Song
"I Love You,
California"

If you want more information,
write to the California Office
of Tourism, 801 K Street,
Suite 1600, Sacramento, CA
95814, 1-800-862-2543.

COLORADO

CAPITAL
Denver

NICKNAME
Centennial State,
Highest State,
or
Switzerland of
America

MOTTO
Nothing without
providence.

BIRD
Lark Bunting

FLOWER
White and Lavender
Columbine

TREE
Blue Spruce

SONG
"Where the
Columbines Grow"

If you want more information,
look in *The Kids' Almanac of
the United States*
(World Almanac).

Connecticut

Capital
Hartford

Nickname
Constitution State,
Nutmeg State,
or
Land of Steady Habits

Motto
He who transplanted
still sustains.

Bird
American Robin

Flower
Mountain Laurel

Tree
White Oak

Song
"Yankee Doodle"

If you want to find out
more about the
geography of the state,
look in an atlas.

DELAWARE

CAPITAL
Dover

NICKNAME
First State,
Peach State,
Small Wonder,
or
Diamond State

MOTTO
Liberty and
independence.

BIRD
Blue Hen Chicken

FLOWER
Peach Blossom

TREE
American Holly

SONG
"Our Delaware"

Use an almanac for
more details about
the state.

Florida

Capital
Tallahassee

Nickname
Sunshine State,
Orange State,
Alligator State,
or
Southernmost State

Motto
In God we trust.

Bird
Mockingbird

Flower
Orange Blossom

Tree
Sabal Palmetto Palm
(Cabbage Palm)

Song
"Old Folks at Home"
✿

Use an encyclopedia
for more details
about the state.

GEORGIA

CAPITAL
Atlanta

NICKNAME
Peach State,
Empire State of the South,
Goober State,
Cracker State,
Buzzard State,
or
Yankee-Land of the South

MOTTO
Wisdom, justice, and
moderation.

BIRD
Brown Thrasher

FLOWER
Cherokee Rose

TREE
Live Oak

SONG
"Georgia on My Mind"
or
"Our Georgia"

Find Dewey Decimal
Classification System section
975.8 on the library shelves for
more details about the state.

Hawaii

Capital
Honolulu

Nickname
Aloha State,
Pineapple State,
Paradise of the Pacific,
or
Youngest State

Motto
The life of the land is
perpetuated in
righteousness.

Bird
Nene (Hawaiian Goose)

Flower
Hibiscus (Yellow)

Tree
Kukui (Candlenut)

Song
"Hawaii Ponoi
(Our Hawaii)"

Use the card or automated
catalog in the library for
materials about the state.

IDAHO

Capital
Boise

Nickname
Gem State,
Gem of the
Mountains,
Spud State,
or
Panhandle State

Motto
It is forever.

Bird
Mountain Bluebird

Flower
Syringa

Tree
White Pine

Song
"Here We Have
Idaho"

Use film and
videotape catalogs
for visual presentations
about the state.

Illinois

Capital
Springfield

Nickname
Land of Lincoln,
Prairie State,
or
Corn State

Motto
State sovereignty,
national union.

Bird
Cardinal

Flower
Native Violet

Tree
White Oak

Song
"Illinois"

Use atlases for
geographical
information
about the state.

©Carolyn S. Brodie, Debra Goodrich, Paula K. Montgomery

Indiana

Capital
Indianapolis

Nickname
Hoosier State

Motto
Crossroads of
America.

Bird
Cardinal

Flower
Peony

Tree
Tulip Tree

Song
"On the Banks of
the Wabash,
Far Away"

Use *Worldmark
Encyclopedia of the
States* for more
information about
the state.

©Carolyn S. Brodie, Debra Goodrich, Paula K. Montgomery

IOWA

CAPITAL
Des Moines

NICKNAME
Hawkeye State,
Land Where the Tall
Corn Grows,
Nation's Breadbasket,
or
Corn State

MOTTO
Our liberties we prize,
and our rights
we will maintain.

BIRD
Eastern Goldfinch

FLOWER
Wild Rose

TREE
Oak

SONG
"The Song of Iowa"

Use periodical indexes
for more information
about the state.

©Carolyn S. Brodie, Debra Goodrich, Paula K. Montgomery

KANSAS

CAPITAL
Topeka

NICKNAME
Sunflower State,
Cyclone State,
Jayhawk State,
or
Squatter State

MOTTO
To the stars through
difficulties.

BIRD
Western Meadowlark

FLOWER
Wild Sunflower

TREE
Cottonwood

SONG
"Home on the Range"
or
"The Kansas March"

Use newspapers for
current information
about events in the state.

©Carolyn S. Brodie, Debra Goodrich, Paula K. Montgomery

Kentucky

Capital
Frankfort

Nickname
Bluegrass State,
Hemp State,
or
Tobacco State

Motto
United we stand,
divided we fall.

Bird
Kentucky Cardinal

Flower
Goldenrod

Tree
Coffee Tree

Song
"Old Kentucky Home"

How can more
information be found?

©Carolyn S. Brodie, Debra Goodrich, Paula K. Montgomery

Louisiana

Capital
Baton Rouge

Nickname
Bayou State,
Sugar State,
Pelican State,
Creole State,
or
Sportsman Paradise

Motto
Union, justice, and
confidence.

Bird
Brown Pelican

Flower
Magnolia

Tree
Bald Cypress

Song
"Give Me Louisiana"
or
"You Are My Sunshine"

Call the State Tourism Office
for more information.

©Carolyn S. Brodie, Debra Goodrich, Paula K. Montgomery

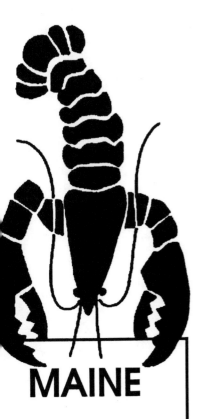

MAINE

Capital
Augusta

Nickname
Pine Tree State,
Lumber State,
Border State,
or
Old Dirigo State

Motto
I Direct.

Bird
Chickadee

Flower
Pine Cone and Tassel

Tree
White Pine

Song
"State of Maine Song"

Look in a gazetteer for
more information about
the state.

©Carolyn S. Brodie, Debra Goodrich, Paula K. Montgomery

MARYLAND

Capital
Annapolis

Nickname
Free State
or
Old-Line State

Motto
Manly deeds,
womanly words.

Bird
Baltimore Oriole

Flower
Black-Eyed Susan

Tree
White Oak

Song
"Maryland,
My Maryland"

What are
the colors in the
Maryland flag?

Look in an
encyclopedia for
information.

©Carolyn S. Brodie, Debra Goodrich, Paula K. Montgomery

Massachusetts

Capital
Boston

Nickname
Bay State,
Old Colony State,
or
Baked Bean State

Motto
By the sword we seek
peace, but peace only
under liberty.

Bird
Chickadee

Flower
Mayflower
(Ground Laurel)

Tree
American Elm

Song
"All Hail to
Massachusetts"
or
"Massachusetts"

Can you find recordings
of Arlo Guthrie's official
folk song for this state?

©Carolyn S. Brodie, Debra Goodrich, Paula K. Montgomery

MICHIGAN

CAPITAL
Lansing

NICKNAME
Wolverine State,
Lake State,
Auto State,
Great Lake State,
or
Lady of the Lake

MOTTO
If you seek a
pleasant penisula,
look about you.

BIRD
Robin

FLOWER
Apple Blossom

TREE
White Pine

SONG
"Michigan, My
Michigan"

Which sources would
help you find out more
about the capital?

Minnesota

Capital
St. Paul

Nickname
North Star State,
Gopher State,
Land of
Ten Thousand Lakes,
or
Bread and Butter State

Motto
The star of the north.

Bird
Loon

Flower
Pink and White
Lady's-Slipper

Tree
Red Pine
(Norway Pine)

Song
"Hail! Minnesota"

Which sources would
help you find
information about the
history of the state?

Mississippi

Capital
Jackson

Nickname
Magnolia State,
Eagle State,
Border-Eagle State,
Bayou State,
or
Mud-Cat State

Motto
By valor and arms.

Bird
Mockingbird

Flower
Magnolia

Tree
Evergreen Magnolia

Song
"Go, Mississippi!"

Which sources would help
you find other symbols of
this state?

Find the subject of symbols
or the name of the state in the
card or automated catalog in
the library to help you in your
search.

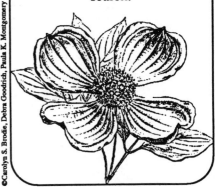

MISSOURI

CAPITAL
Jefferson City

NICKNAME
Show Me State,
Bullion State,
Cave State,
Lead State,
or
Ozark State

MOTTO
The welfare of the people
shall be the supreme law.

BIRD
Bluebird

FLOWER
Hawthorn
(Red Haw Blossom)

TREE
Flowering Dogwood

SONG
"Missouri Waltz"

Which sources would help you find
out about the national sites in this
state? Use the card or automated
catalog in your library to find
materials about the state.

©Carolyn S. Brodie, Debra Goodrich, Paula K. Montgomery

Montana

Capital
Helena

Nickname
Big Sky Country,
Mountain State,
Stub Toe State,
Bonanza State,
or
Treasure State

Motto
Gold and silver.

Bird
Western Meadowlark

Flower
Bitterroot

Tree
Flowering Dogwood

Song
"Montana"
or
"Montana Melody"

Where can you look for
information about people
from this state?
Look for materials in your
library about the state.

©Carolyn S. Brodie, Debra Goodrich, Paula K. Montgomery

Nebraska

Capital
Lincoln

Nickname
Cornhusker State,
Tree Planters' State,
Antelope State,
or
Bug-Eating State

Motto
Equality before the
law.

Bird
Western Meadowlark

Flower
Late Goldenrod

Tree
Cottonwood

Song
"Beautiful Nebraska"

Which sources would
help you locate
information about the
climate of this state?

Look for general
references like
encyclopedias and
geographical
materials in
your library.

©Carolyn S. Brodie, Debra Goodrich, Paula K. Montgomery

NEVADA

CAPITAL
Carson City

NICKNAME
Sage State,
Sagebrush State,
Silver State,
Mining State,
or
Battle-Born State

MOTTO
All for our country.

BIRD
Mountain Bluebird

FLOWER
Sagebrush

TREE
Single-Leaf Pinyon

SONG
"Home Means
Nevada"

What are good sources for
finding out about the
demography or population
of this state?
Find as many sources as
you can in your school or
public library.

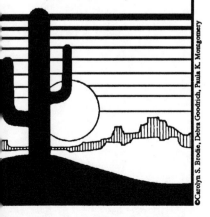

New Hampshire

Capital
Concord

Nickname
Granite State,
White Mountain State,
Switzerland of America,
or
Mother of Rivers

Motto
Live free or die.

Bird
Purple Finch

Flower
Purple Lilac

Tree
White Birch

Song
"Old New Hampshire"
or
"New Hampshire,
My New Hampshire"

Which sources would be
helpful for finding
information about land
use in this state?

Use the resources of your
public library.

NEW JERSEY

Capital
Trenton

Nickname
Garden State,
Clam State,
Camden and Amboy State,
Jersey Blue State,
or
Path of the Revolution

Motto
Liberty and prosperity

Bird
Eastern Goldfinch

Flower
Common
Meadow Violet

Tree
Northern Red Oak

Which source would
help locate information
about the major routes
for transportation
in this state?
Find maps
in the library to help
in your search.

New Mexico

Capital
Santa Fe

Nickname
Cactus State,
Spanish State,
Sunshine State,
or
Land of Enchantment

Motto
It grows as it goes.

Bird
Chaparral Bird
(Roadrunner)

Flower
Yucca Flower

Tree
Nut Pine (Pinon)

Song
"O, Fair New Mexico
(Asi Es Nuevo Mejico)"

Which sources would help locate
information about the people of
this state?

Use the card or automated catalog
in the library for basic information.

©Carolyn S. Brodie, Debra Goodrich, Paula K. Montgomery

New York

Capital
Albany

Nickname
Empire State
or
Excelsior State

Motto
Higher

Bird
Bluebird

Flower
Rose

Tree
Sugar Maple

Although this state
has no official song,
where could taped
versions of good
song possibilities be
found?

Use the catalogs
and indexes in your
library to help locate
versions.

©Carolyn S. Brodie, Debra Goodrich, Paula K. Montgomery

North Carolina

Capital
Raleigh

Nickname
Tarheel State,
Old North State,
or
Turpentine State

Motto
To be rather
than to see.

Bird
Cardinal

Flower
Dogwood

Tree
Pine

Song
"Old North State"

Which sources would be helpful
for learning more about the state
tree and its geographical range?

©Carolyn S. Brodie, Debra Goodrich, Paula K. Montgomery

North Dakota

Capital
Bismarck

Nickname
Sioux State,
Flickertail State,
Land of the Dakotas,
or
Peace Garden State

Motto
Liberty and union now
and forever, one and
inseparable.

Bird
Meadowlark

Flower
Wild Prairie Rose

Tree
American Elm

Song
"North Dakota Hymn"
or
"Spirit of the Land"

Which sources
would be most helpful for
finding more information
about the state bird?
Look for subject
in the card or automated
catalog in the library.

OHIO

CAPITAL
Columbus

NICKNAME
Buckeye State
or
Mother of Modern
Presidents

MOTTO
With God, all things
are possible.

BIRD
Cardinal

FLOWER
Scarlet Carnation

TREE
Buckeye

SONG
"Beautiful Ohio"

Which sources will be
most helpful to find
locations of rivers and
plains in this state?

Look for maps,
atlases, and
geographical materials
in the library.

Oklahoma

Capital
Oklahoma City

Nickname
Sooner State
or
Boomer's Paradise

Motto
Labor conquers
all things.

Bird
Scissor-Tailed
Flycatcher

Flower
Mistletoe

Tree
Redbud

Song
"Oklahoma"

Which sources
would help you
find out about the
automobile
license plates
and laws
of this state?

OREGON

CAPITAL
Salem

NICKNAME
Beaver State,
Web-Foot State,
Sunset State,
Valentine State,
or
Hard-Case State

MOTTO
The union.

BIRD
Western Meadowlark

FLOWER
Oregon Grape

TREE
Douglas Fir

SONG
"Oregon, My Oregon"

Use the card or
automated catalog to
find materials about
fictional characters and
stories set in this state.

Pennsylvania

Capital
Harrisburg

Nickname
Keystone State
or
Quaker State

Motto
Virtue, liberty, and
independence.

Bird
Ruffed Grouse

Flower
Mountain Laurel

Tree
Hemlock

Which sources would be
useful for finding
statistical information
about this state?

Look for the subject in the
card or automated catalog
in the library.

Rhode Island

Capital
Providence
☆
Nickname
Little Rhody,
Smallest State,
Land of Roger Williams,
Plantation State,
or
Ocean State
☆
Motto
Hope
☆
Bird
Rhode Island
Red Chicken
☆
Flower
Violet
☆
Tree
Red Maple
☆
Song
"Rhode Island"
☆
Which sources would be useful
for finding a chronological listing
of important historical events in
this state?
Ask the librarian or library media
specialist for help.

South Carolina

Capital
Columbia

Nickname
Rice State,
Swamp State,
Keystone of the South
Atlantic Seaboard,
Iodine State,
or
Palmetto State

Motto
Prepared in mind and
resources.
or
While I breathe I hope.

Bird
Carolina Wren

Flower
Yellow Jasmine

Tree
Palmetto Tree

Song
"Carolina"
or
"South Carolina
on My Mind"

What
ources
would be
useful for
finding
information
about the
state
seal?

Look for
titles in your
library.

©Carolyn S. Brodie, Debra Goodrich, Paula K. Montgomery

South Dakota

Capital
Pierre

Nickname
Sunshine State,
Coyote State,
Blizzard State,
or
Artesian State

Motto
Under God the
people rule.

Bird
Ring-Necked
Pheasant

Flower
American
Pasqueflower

Tree
Black Hills Spruce

Song
"Hail! South Dakota"

Which sources would be
useful when identifying the
flag of this state?
Look for titles in the library.

©Carolyn S. Brodie, Debra Goodrich, Paula K. Montgomery

Tennessee

Capital
Nashville

Nickname
Volunteer State,
Big Bend State,
or
Mother of Southwestern
Statesmen

Motto
Agriculture
and commerce.

Bird
Mockingbird

Flower
Iris

Tree
Tulip Poplar

Song
"My Homeland,
Tennessee,"
"When It's Iris Time in
Tennessee,"
"My Tennessee,"
"Tennessee Waltz," or
"Rocky Top"

In which sources could
you identify other animal
symbols for this state?

©Carolyn S. Brodie, Debra Goodrich, Paula K. Montgomery

TEXAS

CAPITAL
Austin

NICKNAME
Lone Star State,
Beef State,
or
Banner State

MOTTO
Friendship.

BIRD
Mockingbird

FLOWER
Bluebonnet

TREE
Pecan

SONG
"Texas, Our Texas"
or
"Bluebonnets"

In which sources would
you find names of
authors who have written
fictional works about this
state?

Check the library for
titles.

★★★★★★★★★★★★★★

©Carolyn S. Brodie, Debra Goodrich, Paula K. Montgomery

UTAH

Capital
Salt Lake City

Nickname
Beehive State,
Mormon State,
Land of the Saints,
or
Salt Lake State

Motto
Industry

Bird
Seagull

Flower
Sego Lily

Tree
Blue Spruce

Song
"Utah, We Love
Thee"

Which sources would be
most helpful in finding the
names of the important
historical figures prominent
in the founding of the
state?

Check the library for titles.

©Carolyn S. Brodie, Debra Goodrich, Paula K. Montgomery

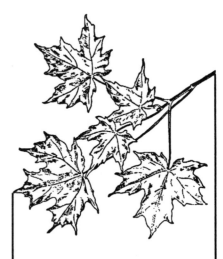

VERMONT

Capital
Montpelier

Nickname
Green Mountain State.

Motto
Freedom and unity

Bird
Hermit Thrush

Flower
Red Clover

Tree
Sugar Maple

Song
"Hail, Vermont!"

In which sources would
the most important
historical events in the
state be listed?

Check the library for titles.

©Carolyn S. Brodie, Debra Goodrich, Paula K. Montgomery

VIRGINIA

CAPITAL
Richmond

NICKNAME
Old Dominion,
Cavalier State,
Mother of Presidents,
or
Mother of States

MOTTO
Thus ever to tyrants.

BIRD
Cardinal

FLOWER
American Dogwood

TREE
American Dogwood

SONG
"Carry Me Back to Old
Virginia"

In which sources would
you locate more
information about this
state's capital?

Look for titles in the
library.

Washington

Capital
Olympia

Nickname
Evergreen State
or
Chinook State

Motto
By and by.

Bird
Willow Goldfinch

Flower
Pink Rhododendron

Tree
Western Hemlock

Song
"Washington,
My Home"

In which sources would
you locate statistical
information about the
population of this
state?

Look in the school or
public library.

West Virginia

Capital
Charleston

Nickname
Mountain State
or
Panhandle State

Motto
Mountaineers
are always free.

Bird
Cardinal

Flower
Rhododendron
(Big or Mountain Laurel)

Tree
Sugar Maple

Song
"This Is My West Virginia,"
"West Virginia, My Home
Sweet Home,"
or
"The West Virginia Hills"

Which sources would help
you locate more information
about the mountains of this state?
Check the school or public
library for resources.

Wisconsin

Capital
Madison

Nickname
Badger State
or
Copper State

Motto
Forward.

Bird
Robin

Flower
Wood Violet

Tree
Sugar Maple

Song
"On, Wisconsin"

Which sources tell
about the economy
of this state?

Visit your library.

WYOMING

CAPITAL
Cheyenne

NICKNAME
Equality State,
Big Wyoming State,
or
Cowboy State

MOTTO
Equal rights.

BIRD
Meadowlark

FLOWER
Indian Paintbrush

TREE
Cottonwood

SONG
"Wyoming"

In which sources could you
find names of the government
officials of this state?

Look for titles in your library.

District of Columbia

Locate these
monuments on a map
of the District of
Columbia. What other
special places can you
locate?

Puerto Rico

Capital
San Juan

Bird
Reinita

Flower
Maga

Tree
Ceiba

Song
"La Borinquena"

What is a good source for maps and geographical information about this island commonwealth? Visit the school or public library.

U.S. Territories

A territory is a part of a nation not accorded statehood or provincial status.

Which names in this list are not U.S. territories?

Kingman Reef
Wake Islands
Guam
Caroline Islands
Puerto Rico
Mariana Islands
U.S. Virgin Islands
Bermuda
Seychelles
American Samoa
Republic of Palau
Baker Island
Howland Island
Jarvis Island
Midway Island
Johnston Atoll

Look in almanacs or other reference materials in the library.

Answer: Seychelles and Bermuda

Preamble of the United Nations Charter

We the peoples of the United Nations determined to save succeeding generations from the scourge of war, which twice in our lifetime has brought untold sorrow to mankind, and
To reaffirm faith in fundamental human rights, in the dignity and worth of the human person, in the equal rights of men and women and of nations large and small, and
To establish conditions under which justice and respect for the obligations arising from treaties and other sources of international law can be maintained, and
To promote social progress and better standards of life in larger freedom, and for these ends
To practice tolerance and live together in peace with one another as good neighbors, and
To unite our strength to maintain international peace and security, and
To insure, by the acceptance of principles and the institution of methods, that armed force shall not be used, save in common interest, and
To employ international machinery for the promotion of the economic and social advancement of all peoples, have resolved to combine our efforts to accomplish these aims.
Accordingly, our respective Governments, through representatives assembled in the city of San Francisco, who have exhibited their full powers found to be in good and due form, have agreed to the present Charter of the United Nations and do hereby establish an international organization to be known as the United Nations.

How many countries are members of the United Nations? (Look it up in a current almanac.)

Copies of the United Nations Charter may be obtained by writing to United Nations Sales Section, United Nations, New York, NY 10017

Bibliography of Sources
on Bookmarks and Ideas

Picture Books

Brown, Laurene Krasny. *Yellow Fish, Blue Fish*. Pictures by Marc Brown. Lexington, MA: Heath, 1989. 64p. (Heath reader includes stories and simple instructions for making bookmarks.)

Fiction Books

Lindbergh, Anne. *Travel Far, Pay No Fare*. New York: HarperCollins, 1992. (A magic bookmark allows two readers to enter stories they read.)

Nonfiction Books

Patterns and ideas may be found in many craft books. These represent examples of sources.

Barkin, Carol, and Elizabeth James. *Happy Valentine's Day*. New York: Lothrop, 1988. pp. 36-37.

Brinn, Ruth E. *More Let's Celebrate*. Rockville, MD: Kar-Ben Copies, 1984. p. 34.

Brown, Ann. *Handmade Christmas Gifts That Are Actually Usable*. Oviedo, FL: Bold Publications, 1987. p. 29.

Brown, Jerome C. *Great Gifts for All Occasions Kids Can Make (For Practically Nothing)*. Belmont, CA: David S. Lake Publications, 1986. pp. 25-26, 41-43.

Cole, Ann, Carolyn Haas, and Betty Weinberger. *Purple Cow to the Rescue*. Boston: Little, Brown, 1982. p. 159.

Conaway, Judith. *Springtime Surprises! Things to Make and Do*. Mahwah, NJ: Troll, 1986. pp. 18-19.

Devonshire, Hillary. *Christmas Crafts*. New York: Watts, 1990. pp. 41-43.

Dobrin, Arnold. *Make a Witch, Make a Goblin: A Book of Halloween Crafts*. New York: Four Winds Press, 1977. p. 79.

Duda, Margaret B. *Useful Gifts Children Can Make*. San Diego, CA: Oak Tree, 1988. pp. 108-9.

Fleishman, Seymour. *Printcrafts for Fun and Profit*. Chicago: A. Whitman, 1977.

Forte, Imogene. *Puddles and Wings and Grapevine Swings*. Nashville, TN: Incentive Publications, 1982. p. 132.

Forte, Imogene. *Rainbow Fun*. Nashville, TN: Incentive Publications, 1987. p. 26.

Glovach, Linda. *The Little Witch's Summertime*. Englewood Cliffs, NJ: Prentice Hall, 1986. pp. 27-28.

Hautzig, Esther. *Make It Special*. New York: Macmillan, 1986. p. 78.

Holiday Crafts Kids Can Make. Des Moines, IA: Meredith, 1987. pp. 102-5.

Holzbauer, Beth. *Creative Crafts for Young Children*. Elgin, IL: Child's World, 1986. p. 54.

Jones, Kathy. *Celebrate Christmas*. Carthage, IL: Good Apple, 1985. p. 103.

Leedy, Loreen. *A Dragon Christmas: Things to Make and Do*. New York: Holiday House, 1988. p. 14.

Lewis, Felicity. *How to Make Presents from Odds and Ends*. New York: Van Nostrand Reinhold, 1972. p. 19.

Lightbody, Donna M. *Let's Knot: A Macrame Book*. New York: Lothrop, Lee and Shepard, 1972.

132 Gift Crafts Kids Can Make. Columbus, OH: Highlights, 1981. pp. 20, 33.

Pettit, Florence Harvey. *The Stamp Pad Printing Book*. New York: Crowell, 1979. pp. 63-70.

Piscitelli, Janice A. *Wings 'n Things: A Handbook of Creative Crafts Activities*. W. Nyack, NY: Parker, 1983. p. 20.

Rasmussen, Richard M., and Linda L. Rasmussen. *The Kids Encyclopedia of Things to Make and Do*. San Diego, CA: Oak Tree, 1981. pp. 24, 94-95.

Supraner, Robyn. *Fun with Paper*. Mahwah, NJ: Troll, 1981. pp. 18-19.

———. *Happy Halloween: Things to Make and Do*. Mahwah, NJ: Troll, 1981. pp. 20-21.

———. *Valentine's Day: Things to Make and Do*. Mahwah, NJ: Troll, 1981.

Thanksgiving Handbook. Elgin, IL: Child's World, 1985. p. 58.

Volpe, Nancee. *Good Apple and Seasonal Arts and Crafts*. Carthage, IL: Good Apple, 1982. pp. 79, 110.

Wolfe, Marcia. *Easy Crafts for Children*. Cincinnati, OH: Standard, 1985. pp. 32, 38.

Periodical Articles for Students

Pack O'Fun. See the following issues' dates and pages: Summer 1981, p. 44; Summer 1982, p. 45; Fall 1982, p. 18; Spring 1985, p. 7; Spring 1990, p. 4, 10; Summer 1990, p. 6; January/February 1991, p. 31.

Periodical Articles for Professionals

Conroy, Michael T. "Project Bookmark: Reading and Graphic Arts." *Journal of Reading* 15:1 (October 1971), pp. 60-61.

Isleib, Carol M. "Bookmark Treasures." *Handwoven* 13:3 (May 1, 1992), p. 74.

"Plastic-Canvas Bookmark and Key Chain." *Crafts 'n Things* 18:3 (December 1, 1992), p. 60.

Schwartz, Judith D. "Alfred Knopf Revives the Classics of Children's Literature." *Brandweek* 33:45 (November 30, 1992), pp. 26-27.

"Small Stuff: Quick and Easy Projects to Make and Give with Love." *Crafts 'n Things* 19:6 (April 6, 1994), p. 86. (Cross-Stitch Bookmark)

Poetry About Bookmarks

Kanyadi, Sandor, and Len Roberts. "Bookmark." *The American Poetry Review* 19:5 (September-October 1990), p. 29.

Shaw, Robert B. "The Bookmark." *Poetry*. 155:6 (March 1990), p. 395.